D1617483

Managing by Objectives

Management Applications Series

Alan C. Filley, University of Wisconsin, Madison
Series Editor

Performance in Organizations: Determinants and Appraisal
L. L. Cummings, University of Wisconsin, Madison
Donald P. Schwab, University of Wisconsin, Madison

Leadership and Effective Management
Fred E. Fiedler, University of Washington
Martin M. Chemers, University of Utah

Managing by Objectives
Anthony P. Raia, University of California, Los Angeles

Organizational Change: Techniques and Applications
Newton Margulies, University of California, Irvine
John C. Wallace, University of California, Irvine

Interpersonal Conflict Resolution
Alan C. Filley, University of Wisconsin, Madison

*Group Techniques for Program Planning: A Guide to Nominal
  Group and Delphi Processes*
Andre L. Delbecq, University of Wisconsin, Madison
Andrew H. Van de Ven, Kent State University
David H. Gustafson, University of Wisconsin, Madison

Organizational Behavior Modification
Fred Luthans, University of Nebraska, Lincoln
Robert Kreitner, Western Illinois University

Managing by Objectives

Anthony P. Raia

University of California, Los Angeles

HD
38
.R163
WEST

ASU WEST LIBRARY

A15012 090395

Scott, Foresman and Company
Glenview, Illinois   Brighton, England

Library of Congress Catalog Number: 73-80986
ISBN: 0-673-07757-8.

Copyright © 1974 Scott, Foresman and Company, Glenview, Illinois.
Philippines Copyright 1974 Scott, Foresman and Company.
All Rights Reserved.
Printed in the United States of America.

Regional offices of Scott, Foresman and Company are located in Dallas,
Texas; Glenview, Illinois; Oakland, New Jersey; Palo Alto, California;
Tucker, Georgia; and Brighton, England.

Foreword

The Management Applications Series is concerned with the application of contemporary research, theory, and techniques. There are many excellent books at advanced levels of knowledge, but there are few which address themselves to the application of such knowledge. The authors in this series are uniquely qualified for this purpose, since they are all scholars who have experience in implementing change in real organizations through the methods they write about.

Each book treats a single topic in depth. Where the choice is between presenting many approaches briefly or a single approach thoroughly, we have opted for the latter. Thus, after reading the book, the student or practitioner should know how to apply the methodology described.

Selection of topics for the series was guided by contemporary relevance to management practice, and by the availability of an author qualified as an expert, yet able to write at a basic level of understanding. No attempt is made to cover all management methods, nor is any sequence implied in the series, although the books do complement one another. For example, change methods might fit well with managing by objectives.

The books in this series may be used in several ways. They may be used to supplement textbooks in basic courses on management, organizational behavior, personnel, or industrial psychology/sociology. Students appreciate the fact that the material is immediately applicable. Practicing managers will want to use individual books to increase their skills, either through self study or in connection with management development programs, inside or outside the organization.

Alan C. Filley

Preface

This book is an attempt to provide a clear understanding of the fundamental concepts and tools required to design and implement an effective MBO system. It is based upon existing management theory, research, and experience. As such, it reflects my view of the current state of both the science and the art of managing by objectives. This book is specifically intended to provide a comprehensive but concise view of the concept; to develop a systematic approach to MBO; and to show students and practitioners how to use this approach to management.

The book itself is divided into nine chapters. The first chapter places the managerial job in perspective and sets the stage for management by objectives. Chapter 2 provides a conceptual overview and presents a model or framework which views MBO as a system rather than as a technique of management.

The remaining chapters treat each of the major elements of the model in greater detail. The emphasis of Chapter 3 is on setting goals and objectives for the organization and its subunits, while Chapter 4 focuses on setting job objectives for the individual manager. Examples, guidelines, and sample forms are also provided to illustrate how long-range goals, strategic plans, organizational performance objectives, and individual job objectives are derived and related to each other.

Chapter 5 discusses action planning as a way of developing the means for achieving objectives. Included are descriptions of some methods and techniques which can be used to clarify responsibility and authority relationships. The concept of "self-control" is made operational in Chapter 6 where some of the better-known theories of motivation are discussed and related to participative MBO systems as a way of getting commitment for accomplishments and results.

The focus of Chapter 7 is on progressive reviews and performance appraisals. Illustrations and guidelines are provided to facilitate the appraisal process. Chapter 8 explains how key activities such as manager training, compensation, and career and manpower planning can be integrated into the MBO system.

The final chapter uses several case studies to illustrate how an MBO system might be installed and distills guidelines and suggestions for its implementation from them. The annotated bibliography included at the end of the book provides a summary of what has been written on the subject and a ready reference list for those who might like to go into some aspect of the subject in greater detail.

Many people generally contribute to the creation of a book. This one is no exception. I owe a debt of gratitude to my colleagues and friends who, through their involvement in our MBO seminars, have greatly influenced my thinking and approach to the subject. I am also indebted to many managers who helped me develop and refine some of these concepts on the hard rocks of reality. A special note of thanks is due to Mrs. Helen Schwartz for typing the final manuscript and helping me meet the deadlines.

Anthony P. Raia

Contents

Managing by Objectives

Management
in Perspective

1

INTRODUCTION

This is a book about management. More specifically, it is about a management philosophy and style which has captured the fancy of many academicians, consultants, and practitioners in the field. It is a demanding and rewarding way of managing the resources of an organization. As such, it represents a pragmatic and practical approach to dealing with many of the problems confronting the manager today. The approach is not new. The last decade, in fact, has seen the rise of a great tide of praise and criticism in the literature.

Like almost everything else in the world, "management by objectives" comes in all sizes, all colors, and all shapes. Academicians and consultants have packaged and sold it under many different labels, a few of which are "management by results," "management by objectives and results," "management by goals and results," and "individual goal-setting." And practitioners have spawned "goals and controls (GAC)," "work planning and review (WPR)," "objectives, strategies, and tactics (OST)," "charter of accountability concept—Hughes (COACH)," and a host of other acronymic, personal recipes. Their applications include providing a basis for an objective performance appraisal system, facilitating managerial planning and control, helping train and develop managers, providing the basis for incentive compensation, and increasing the level of involvement and degree of participation in the management of the affairs of the organization. Many current programs have integrated some combination of these managerial activities with varying degrees of success. Consequently, "management by objectives" has been steadily maturing as a way of life for many managers in a wide variety of organizations.

This book is essentially an attempt to provide a clear understanding of the managing by objectives concept. It develops a systemic and systematic framework and approach. Although illustrations and guidelines are provided throughout, no attempt is made to provide a universally applicable system or model. *There is no one best way to manage by objectives!* Each system, each program, must fit the needs and circumstances of a given organization. The object of this book is to provide the kinds of insights and understanding that it takes to successfully develop and implement a management by objectives system in *any* organization. An overview of the conceptual framework which describes the system is presented in the next chapter. Subsequent chapters deal with each major element of the model in greater depth. The emphasis throughout is on both theory and practice. The management of change and the problems associated with installing the system are presented in the final chapter. A rather comprehensive annotated bibliography has been included as a guide for those who wish to pursue some aspect of the subject matter in greater detail.

The remaining portions of this chapter reflect an attempt to provide some perspectives on the role and process of management in organizations. They have been included to provide us with a common frame of reference and a foundation upon which to build. Admittedly, we might have used any one of a number of different theories or approaches to the manager's job. Some tend to stress quantitative methods and mathematical analysis; they focus on the manager as a rational problem-solver and decision-maker. Some deal primarily with the human aspects of organizational life; they tend to focus on the manager as a leader and motivator. Some tend to emphasize the administrative functions of management; they focus on the manager as one who plans, organizes, and controls the activities of other people. And some approaches apply systems theory to management in organizations and tend to focus on the manager as a creator and operator of a sociotechnical system.

The framework which follows has been selected for a number

of reasons. First, it provides a common language and a way of relating the process of management to the concept of managing by objectives. When viewed in their totality, the activities listed below make up the process. Second, the framework is eclectic—it incorporates many of the relevant parts of the different approaches and recognizes that they are equally important. Third, the focus is on what managers actually *do* in organizations. The functions and activities selected are those which appear most frequently in the literature and are easily related to the manager's job. Finally, and perhaps most importantly, most students and practitioners of management are already familiar with the concepts and terms used. Consequently, they will not be faced with the task of having to learn a new language or to "put old wine in new bottles."

THE ROLE OF MANAGEMENT

Management is the dynamic force which converts human and nonhuman resources into organizations. It is a process which integrates previously unrelated resources into something that is greater than the mere sum of its parts. While the purpose of management is to coordinate the activities of people in organizations, its overall role is to facilitate the effective and efficient attainment of organizational goals and the personal needs of its members.

Conventional approaches to managing rely heavily on the organization chart and its associated position descriptions, which generally depict what an individual is responsible for. They do not reflect what the manager does or accomplishes. The organization is seen as a structure of responsibilities and a structure of authority to make decisions. As the organization grows in size, further division of labor becomes necessary. That is, the subunits are further divided, allowing each manager to delegate some of his authority, while retaining his responsibility.

A structure of authority is also required to ensure the fulfillment of these responsibilities and to provide for coordination between the different parts of the organization. Starting at the lowest level, the manager of each part is responsible upward to the manager at the next higher level and, within defined limits, has authority downward over his subunit. The result is a clear and distinct chain of responsibility and authority that tells who interacts with whom in terms of compliance and command. Since changes can be effected only by a formal reorganization of these relationships, conventional approaches tend to take a static view of management.

Modern managers, on the other hand, know that the organization represents something more than a formal framework and a set of task-oriented relationships. They know that members do not carry out their prescribed roles and assignments exactly as planned; social interactions strongly affect work relationships. They know that communications do not always flow through designated channels; informal networks and "grapevines" become important elements in an organization's information system. They know that authority never in fact fully equals responsibility; a manager at any level of the organization is held accountable for things that he cannot directly control. They know that decisions are not always made in accordance with the formal hierarchy; a personal power structure develops which may or may not coincide with the designated centers of authority. The result of these unplanned interactions is a complex pattern of task and interpersonal relationships which operates simultaneously around the formal framework. Management must not only create and maintain the organizational structure, but must understand and learn to deal with the resulting complexity of the *total* environment, one that is becoming more and more turbulent every day. How, then, can we describe the manager's job?

Management is getting things done through people.

Everyone has some conception of the manager's job. At least intuitively, almost everyone is aware that it involves abilities and skills quite different from those which are needed to do the work that is being managed. Perhaps this definition has some merit. It is simple and it focuses on the relationships between managers and people. It does not, however, help us understand management as the coordinating force in organizations. Management also involves determining *where* the organization is going, *what* things need to be done to help it get there, *how* they are to be achieved, *who* is to achieve them, and by *when*. The emphasis is most certainly on *getting things done*.

> The overall job of the manager is to create within the enterprise an environment which will facilitate the accomplishment of its objective. . . . In doing this, the manager plans the operations of his subordinates, selects and trains them, organizes their role relationships, directs their work, and evaluates the results (Koontz and O'Donnell, 1972).

This description has merit in that the emphasis is on creating an environment designed to facilitate the attainment of objectives. Implicit in descriptions of this type, however, are the notions that managers do only managerial work and that nonmanagers do not perform managerial functions. Neither is true. Managers very often engage in nonmanagerial activities and, conversely, some managerial functions are actually performed by nonmanagers. There are many people in any given organization who play an active and vital role in the process of management. More simply stated, management involves getting things done *with* other people.

> The essential task of modern management is to deal with change. Management is the agency through which most changes enter our society, and it is the agency that then must cope with the environment it has set in turbulent motion (Ways, 1966).

The accelerating rate of change in modern America profoundly affects our social institutions. Organizations are faced not only with innovations in science and technology, but also with changing values concerning the nature of man. The result has been great change in management processes. Older mechanistic organizational structures are gradually giving way to newer matrix forms and more organic temporary systems. Managerial authority based upon "delegated" rights is gradually giving way to the authority of knowledge and competence. Institutional power based on coercion and threat is gradually giving way to power based upon collaboration and reason. The concept of man as an inert instrument to be manipulated and controlled by the organization has become obsolete. The depersonalized values of bureaucratic institutions are gradually being replaced by organizational values based upon humanistic and democratic ideals.

Modern management, then, is a dynamic process which involves change. Today's managers require a high capacity for dealing with the complexities of a turbulent and changing environment, for identifying opportunities and priorities, for defining appropriate problems and isolating their causes, for mobilizing the organization's resources, and for initiating the required actions. They are generally responsible for defining (and redefining) the missions and purposes of their organizations. They are also responsible for translating them into verifiable goals and seeing that these are achieved. The modern manager tends to be both goal-oriented and achievement-oriented.

For the professional manager, the magnitude of role conflict is likely to increase in one way, for the environment of the modern manager is more dynamic, turbulent, and clogged than that of his counterpart operating in the relatively stable and more certain world of the nineteenth century (McGregor, 1967).

The manager's job, then, is both complex and changing. He is faced with the task of continuously redefining his role and activities in the light of changing circumstances. His responsibilities are diverse, but his authority is fuzzy and unclear. The claims on his time and energy are severe. He can no longer respond to all of the demands and pressures placed upon him. Unless he has a clear idea of where he is going and how he plans to get there, frustration is inevitable. He can ill afford to stand around waiting for something to happen or for someone to tell him what to do.

KEY FUNCTIONS AND ACTIVITIES

Those descriptions of management most useful to the practitioner tend to concentrate on the activities or functions actually performed by managers. Most lists tend to be arbitrary and reflect differences in emphasis rather than content. Some, for example, stress basic functions like planning, organizing, and controlling; others may focus on the decision-making aspects of management or the importance of leadership and motivation. If management is to be seen in its proper perspective, however, adequate attention must be given to each of these elements.

Planning, organizing, controlling, decision-making, and leadership have been generally identified among the more important functions of management. It should be noted first that these distinctions are made for analytical purposes only. They do not represent separate and distinct activities, but rather interrelated and interdependent processes in the overall managerial process. Further, there is no special order in which they take place. The list simply enables us to look at a complex phenomenon in a systematic way and helps us to focus attention on certain key activities essential to the total job of management in organizations.

Planning and organizational control

Planning and control are perhaps the most basic and pervasive of all managerial functions. Planning is essentially an intellectual activity which involves setting goals and determining how they are to be achieved. It renders human behavior in organizations less random and unpredictable. It gives direction and purpose to an organization's activities. As someone once said, "If you don't know where you're going, any road will get you there." Organizational controls, on the other hand, seek to ensure that plans are being followed. They are often expressed as specific measures or standards of performance. The signal for corrective action generally comes from a deviation from the standard.

Planning and control are inseparable elements in the management process. One is the prerequisite of the other. Planning specifies organizational objectives and activities; control is concerned with how well they have been accomplished. Together they enable the manager to deal with uncertainty and change and help him influence the future. The manager who does not plan, or plans poorly, soon finds himself engaged in "management by crisis." Most of his time is spent fighting fires and dealing with problems which might otherwise have been avoided. He has precious little time left for creating opportunities which contribute to the growth and development of his organization.

Organizing

As a managerial activity, organizing involves creating and staffing the formal structure of work relationships in the organization. It is primarily concerned with establishing effective relationships between tasks and people. The process itself involves several key steps: determining the major functions or activities that must be performed to meet planned goals; dividing them into manageable positions or tasks; grouping and relating the activities in some logical manner; and selecting appropriate people to do the work.

Depending upon the size and complexity of the organization, dividing the work in this manner creates a need for vertical and horizontal coordination. Consequently, appropriate centers of authority and adequate channels of communication must also be provided. The end result is an activity-authority structure which facilitates the process by which work assignments are made and carried out by individual members of the organization.

It should be noted that the process is not as mechanical as it may appear. People are generally selected and trained to fill certain positions or to perform specified tasks. On the other hand, there are many instances where the content of the job and its relationship to the rest of the organization are defined in terms of the skills and personality of a given individual. The manager who does not build an appropriate organizational structure finds himself enmeshed in a chaotic environment. While a sound structure does not guarantee effective working relationships, a poor one makes good relationships impossible.

Decision-making

Decision-making is the focus of most managerial activities. All of us make decisions which have direct implications for our own behavior. The manager, however, makes decisions that are intended to influence the behavior of others.

In its most simple form, decision-making is a logical and rational process of identifying objectives or goals and creating and choosing among alternative strategies or means for achieving them. Making sound managerial decisions, however, is not a simple matter; many factors must be weighed according to the best available information, whether fact or guess. In the latter event, it is more an art than a science.

The making of decisions is fundamental to the process of management. As a decision-maker, the manager must translate problems and opportunities into specific goals that he wishes to attain, develop creative alternative strategies or means for achieving them, and assess the various environmental factors which, together with the strategy he selects, will determine the consequences for him and his organization. No small part of his job is devoted to making decisions, either as an individual or working with groups involved in one or more of the steps in the process.

Motivation and self-control

In the process of management, leadership is generally concerned with creating a motivating work environment. It is aimed at influencing or changing the behavior of people. It is also aimed at creating an environment in which organization members exercise a high degree of control over their own behavior. Unlike organizational control, which is part of the external work environment, both motivation and self-control operate *within* an individual. This generally occurs when organizational goals and individual needs are compatible—when individual needs are satisfied by working on tasks related to organizational goals. Organizations tend to be most successful when the needs of its members are properly integrated with its goals and objectives.

As a leader, the manager's job is to provide for the simultaneous satisfaction of multiple and often conflicting goals and needs, but this is easier said than done. Modern man is extremely complex; his abilities and motives vary considerably. The good leader is sensitive to this and is able to see and feel things from the points of view of others; he is aware of his own attitudes and assumptions and how they affect his behavior in dealing with people; and he has the personal flexibility to vary his behavior in appropriate ways.

The manager, like the leader, should use the human resources in his organization in a way that utilizes their initiative and creativity. He should provide them with an opportunity to grow and develop to their full potential, and in so doing motivate them beyond the levels of minimum performance. Good leaders are not necessarily good managers, but good managers most certainly are good leaders.

The identification and development of goals is implicit in each of the above key management functions and activities. Planning, for example, involves establishing goals and determining the means for their attainment. The formal structure of task roles and relationships is generally based upon planned goals. The identification of goals is also a first and essential element of managerial decision-making. Motivation and self-control generally involve the integration of human needs with organizational goals. The identification and development of goals, then, is the common thread that seems to tie them all together. One can easily see why managing goals and objectives is at the very core of the process of management in organizations.

REFERENCES

Koontz, H., and C. O'Donnell. *Principles of Management: An Analysis of Managerial Functions.* McGraw-Hill, 1972, p. 46.

McGregor, D. *The Professional Manager.* McGraw-Hill, 1967, p. 55.

Ways, M. "Tomorrow's management: A more adventurous life in a free-form corporation." *Fortune* (July 1, 1966): 84.

A Conceptual Overview

2

MANAGING BY OBJECTIVES

Overall organizational goals, properly developed and applied, play an important role in the success of any enterprise. Not only do they provide the basis for the selection of resources, but they guide the formulation of long- and short-range plans, policies, and procedures. From them are distilled the criteria used to appraise the organization's performance and progress.

Specific goals provide the parameters which help guide the daily operations of the firm. The various activities assumed by different individuals at different times are more likely to be consistent if the organization's goals are clearly stated and understood. Moreover, unless precise subgoals and objectives are provided, individual efforts may not contribute to the overall aims of the organization.

Regardless of their clarity, however, basic goals need to be translated into specific objectives that are tangible and meaningful to the day-to-day activities of the organization. The process of assigning a part of a major role to a particular department, and then further subdividing the assignment among sections and individuals, creates what might be called a hierarchy of objectives and subobjectives, the objec-

10

tives of each subunit contributing to those of the larger unit of which it is a part.

The process is complicated somewhat by the dynamic nature of the internal and external environments. Specific assignments to particular individuals are derived from organizational goals which are neither static nor automatic. Fluctuations in the operating environment may call for major revisions and will consequently require adjustments in the hierarchy.

The very essence of management involves coordinating the activities of people toward the attainment of these objectives. One of the principal tasks of the manager, then, is to define and interpret clearly the broad organizational goals, a process involving the development of a hierarchy of objectives to integrate individual activities into an expression of organizational purpose. The proper integration of these objectives, however, involves both an understanding and an acceptance of them by the individuals concerned.

Management theory and practice have spawned a wide variety of techniques and programs designed to facilitate the goal-setting process in organizations. Management by objectives (MBO) is perhaps among the best known. As indicated earlier, it has been applied in one form or another in many business firms, government agencies, school systems, and universities. What is MBO? How does it work? Although the concept itself is both logical and simple, it is difficult to describe in only one dimension or in simple terms.

Management by objectives is, first of all, a *philosophy* of management. It is a philosophy which reflects a "proactive" rather than a "reactive" way of managing. The emphasis is on trying to predict and influence the future rather than on responding and reacting by the seat of the pants. It is also a "results-oriented" philosophy of management, one which emphasizes accomplishments and results. The focus is generally on change and on improving both individual and organizational effectiveness. It is a philosophy which encourages increased participation in the management of the affairs of the organization at all levels. Its "participative management" style is one which is consistent with the needs and demands of a modern society.

Management by objectives is also a *process* consisting of a series of interdependent and interrelated steps: (1) the formulation of clear, concise statements of objectives; (2) the development of realistic action plans for their attainment; (3) the systematic monitoring and measuring of performance and achievement; and (4) the taking of the corrective actions necessary to achieve the planned results. The key elements in the process are "goal setting," "action planning," "self-control," and "periodic progress reviews."

Finally, management by objectives is a *system* of management designed to facilitate planning and organizational control, organizing and assigning tasks, problem-solving and decision-making, and motivation and self-control, as well as other important management functions and activities. It is a system which lets some of the things an organization is already doing (perhaps chaotically) be done in a logical and systematic way. Activities such as performance appraisal, manager development, compensation, and manpower planning can be meaningfully integrated into the system. The rest of this chapter is devoted to tracing the evolution of the concept and to providing a conceptual overview of MBO as a philosophy, a process, and a system of management.

THE EVOLUTION OF MBO

Peter F. Drucker (1954) is generally credited with providing the first definitive statement of the MBO philosophy and process. The job of management, according to him, is to balance a variety of needs and goals "in every area [market standing, innovation, productivity, physical and financial resources, profitability, manager performance and development, worker performance and attitude, and public responsibility] where performance and results directly and vitally affect the survival and prosperity of the business." The first requirement in the task of managing is "management by objectives and self-control," a process requiring each manager, himself, to establish the objectives for his department or unit. The objectives must be defined in terms of their contribution to the larger unit of which he is a part, with higher management having the right to approve them. To ensure that the goals are consistent with the purpose of the enterprise, each manager also responsibly participates in the development of the objectives of the higher unit.

Participation in the goal-setting process makes it possible for the manager to control his own performance. To do this, however, he must be able to measure performance and results against his objectives. These measurements need not be rigidly quantitative, nor exact, but they must be clear and rational. Self-control, coupled with clearly defined objectives, is presumed to lead to greater motivation on the part of the individual manager.

Edward C. Schleh (1961) describes "management by results," a slightly modified version of the original MBO concept. This approach is based upon the belief that better organizational performance is directly related to the extent to which its objectives are stated in terms of final measurable results. The aim of this technique is "to integrate the work of the individual toward the overall objectives of the institution with his own personal interests and desires." According to Schleh, individuals may easily lose sight of the central purpose of the enterprise if only the activities which are required of them are specified. Management objectives must be expressed in terms of the specific accomplishments or results expected from each individual manager if activities are to be effectively coordinated.

The process differs somewhat from that originally described by Drucker. Goal setting is seen as essentially the job of the superior and is "the final expression of his delegation" of authority. He consults with his subordinates before establishing the results expected of them in an attempt to integrate individual objectives with those of the organization. Schleh also advocates self-control for effective management by results. As long as a deviation is within the man's scope of authority, "the control plan should report deviations to the manager himself, not to his superior."

The late Douglas McGregor (1960) proposed a slightly modified, grass-roots approach to MBO. His concept of "management by integration and self-control" was based upon the assumption that people will exercise self-direction and self-control in the attainment of organizational goals to the degree that they are committed to them. According to McGregor, the work of professional managers is essentially a "creative intellectual effort" and the management of such work consists chiefly of establishing objectives or goals and obtaining the professional's commitment to them.

Genuine commitment, he thought, is based upon the principle of integration. This principle demands that both the organization's and the individual's goals must be recognized. It involves the "creation of conditions such that the members of the organization can achieve their own goals *best* by directing their efforts toward the success of the enterprise."

Management by integration and self-control, then, is a slight modification of the concept as originally proposed by Drucker. Its primary aim is to encourage the proper integration of enterprise purpose and personal goals. This is presumably accomplished through the active and responsible participation in the process of the subordinate manager. The overall methodology is similar to those previously discussed, except in that the goals are established by the subordinate rather than by the superior. The superior's role in the process is essentially one of consultation and consists chiefly of assisting the subordinate manager in establishing realistic goals for his area of responsibility. The individual then exercises self-control in much the same manner, and presumably with the same benefits, as described earlier.

The actual application of the concept of MBO in organizations over the past decade or so has evolved through three distinct phases:

Phase 1: Performance appraisal

During the early stages of its application, MBO programs were narrowly focused on evaluating the performance of managers. The emphasis was on developing objective criteria and standards of performance for individuals in a given job. This was due primarily to management's dissatisfaction with the traditional approaches to performance appraisal, which for the most part attempted to evaluate people on the basis of their personality traits. The manager was placed in the uncomfortable and untenable position of trying to judge the personal worth of his subordinates (for an excellent presentation of this view, see McGregor, 1957). MBO offers a sounder approach in that the subordinate actively participates in the process of setting objective performance goals and in appraising his own progress toward them.

As a result of this emphasis, Phase 1 MBO programs have developed a number of distinguishing characteristics. First, and perhaps foremost, they are generally only mildly supported by top management. Leadership and responsibility for the program essentially comes from the personnel department. Line management involvement is essentially limited to filling out the forms and following the procedures established by members of the personnel department. Performance reviews are conducted once a year and generally involve only the subordinate and his immediate superior. Because it is a logical and relatively easy way to begin, performance appraisal still provides the basis for the introduction of many MBO programs. They may tend to become less effective, however, if they retain the above characteristics and do not move beyond to the other phases.

Phase 2: Planning and control

As the application of the concept expanded during the late 1960s, programs began to change. A much broader view prevailed. The emphasis was on incorporating MBO into the organization's planning and control process. Objectives became tied to plans which in turn provided the basis for control through budgets. Performance appraisal was still an essential element in the program. Consequently, Phase 2 MBO programs tend to reflect characteristics other than those described above. First, there is considerably more top management interest and support. Second, the impetus and responsibility for the program comes from line management with strong support from the personnel department. Third, the program generally is tied to the organization's planning and budgeting cycle which usually covers a period of one year. And fourth, there is increased emphasis on the training and development of subordinates.

Phase 3: Integrative management systems

Within the past few years MBO has emerged as a system designed to integrate key management processes and activities in a logical and consistent manner. These include the development of overall organizational goals and strategic plans, problem-solving and decision-making, performance appraisal, executive compensation, manpower planning, and management training and development. The characteristics of integrative MBO systems are very different from those described above: The direction and thrust come from top management, but managers at all levels are actively involved in the process; the increased need for "teamwork" involves more groups in establishing goals, action planning, and reviewing performance; goal setting is more flexible and covers longer time spans; there are more frequent performance reviews; and there is more emphasis on individual growth and development.

THE MBO PROCESS

As indicated earlier, managing by objectives involves a series of interrelated elements. These are summarized in Figure 2–1. The essential elements in the MBO process include:

FIGURE 2-1. The MBO Process.

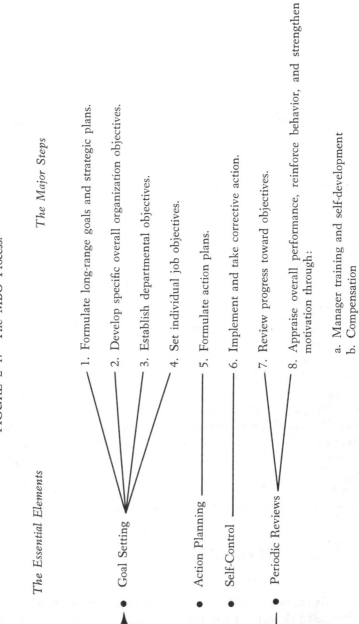

The Essential Elements

The Major Steps

1. Formulate long-range goals and strategic plans.
2. Develop specific overall organization objectives.
3. Establish departmental objectives.
4. Set individual job objectives.
5. Formulate action plans.
6. Implement and take corrective action.
7. Review progress toward objectives.
8. Appraise overall performance, reinforce behavior, and strengthen motivation through:

   a. Manager training and self-development
   b. Compensation
   c. Career and manpower planning

Goal Setting

Action Planning

Self-Control

Periodic Reviews

RECYCLE

Goal setting

The heart of managing by objectives lies in establishing tangible, measurable, and verifiable objectives in key areas of performance. Although overall organizational goals generally constitute a starting point, a distinction is made between those goals which are specific targets (e.g., the rate of return for a given period) and those nebulous statements which remain unchanged from year to year (e.g., "sound customer relations"). Once specific overall goals have been established, the step-by-step process of translating them into required action throughout the organization begins.

Upper-level managers formulate the specific objectives they plan to attain. These are generally concerned with each manager's (or group's) own area of responsibility and are consequently somewhat narrower in scope than the overall organizational goals. Once approved by top management, the objectives of each manager are communicated by him to his subordinates. The subordinates, in turn, go through essentially the same procedure of translating their superiors' goals into required action and formulating objectives in their own areas of responsibility. Once again, the goals of each subordinate manager represent only a part of his superior's goals, are narrower in scope, are more detailed, and generally cover a shorter time period. The process is repeated at every level of management until a clear and integrated hierarchy of objectives exists throughout the entire organization.

Action planning

While a clear set of objectives reflects the "ends" of managerial performance, well-conceived action plans provide the "means" for their attainment. Action planning involves determining *what, who, when, where,* and *how much* is needed to achieve a given objective. It is a practical way of providing a connecting link between the statement of an objective and a more complete program of implementation.

Self-control

Inherent in the process is the notion that the individual, not his superior, will control his own behavior and the activities required to implement the action plan and to achieve the objective. Self-control requires meaningful participation in the goal-setting and action-planning process, resulting in a better understanding and a higher level of commitment to the objectives. The individual must also, however, be given the feedback and information he needs to assess progress and to take corrective action on his own.

Periodic reviews

Systematic reviews designed to assess progress and performance in terms of the established objectives are fundamental to the success of the process. Problem areas are identified and obstacles removed so that additional levels of success and new objectives can be established. Periodic reviews, or "coaching" sessions, should be held as frequently as practicable during the goal period. They may be conducted on a one-on-one basis or in small groups.

The above elements are brought to life and tied together by a series of interdependent activities. The dynamics of the process itself are the result of the following iterative steps:

Step 1

Formulate long-range goals and strategic plans. These are generally based upon a critical review and analysis of the fundamental purpose of the enterprise. "Why does the organization exist?" "What kind of an organization is it?" "What kind of an organization is it trying to become?" Strategic planning helps to identify those areas needing improvement of performance and results.

Step 2

Develop the specific objectives to be achieved within the given time period. These are generally in key areas which reflect overall organizational performance. For the business enterprise, for example, objectives would be established for profitability, productivity, market standing, and areas similar to those outlined by Drucker (1954).

Step 3

Establish derivative objectives and subobjectives for major departments and subunits. For example, overall productivity goals may be further defined by the production department in terms of such things as number of units produced per product or product line, volume of scrap or waste, inventory levels and cost, and numerous other measures of performance.

Step 4

Set realistic and challenging objectives and standards of performance for members of the organization. These are generally aimed at improving individual or group performance in terms of key result activities, problem-solving activities, and innovative or creative activities. Personal growth and development objectives may also be included in the goal statements.

Step 5

Formulate action plans for achieving the stated objectives. This essentially involves specifying the activities or the events which must logically occur to achieve the objectives effectively and efficiently.

Step 6

Implement and take corrective action when required to ensure the attainment of objectives. Necessary for this step are the existence of criteria and standards against which to measure performance, a relevant data base and feedback loops, and whatever other mechanisms are required to facilitate self-control.

Step 7

Review individual and organizational performance in terms of established goals and objectives. This involves periodic, systematic reviews to measure and discuss progress, identify and resolve problems,

FIGURE 2–2.   MBO as a System.

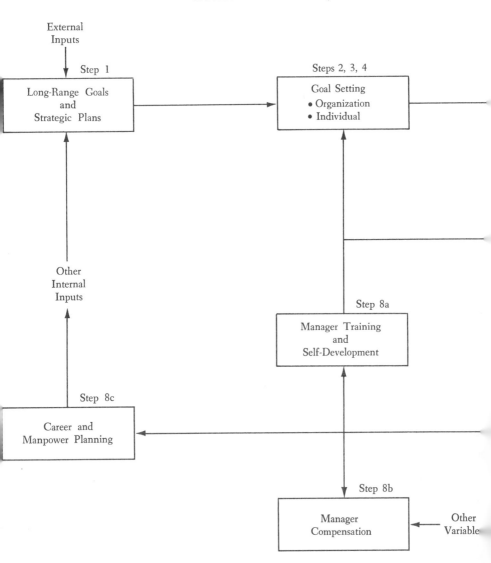

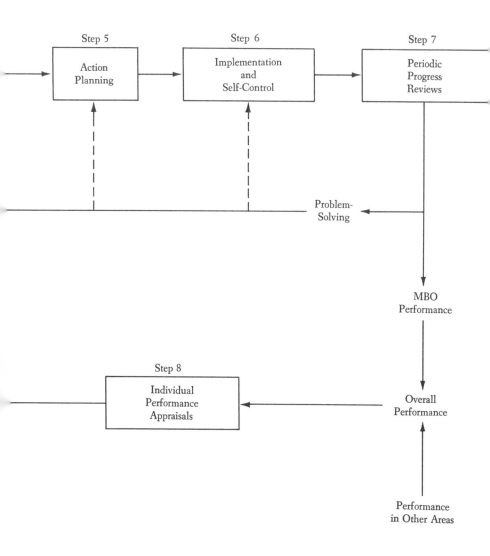

and revise objectives and priorities as may be required by new or additional information.

Step 8

Appraise overall performance, reinforce behavior, and strengthen motivation through effective management training and development, compensation, and career planning. This step is essential to the effective development of human resources and must be made an explicit part of the MBO process.

MBO AS A SYSTEM

Management by objectives is not a procedural or cookbook approach to managing; it is more than just a management tool or technique. It is a way of integrating the key managerial processes and activities in a logical and meaningful way. A conceptual overview of management by objectives as a system is presented in Figure 2–2. The major elements and steps in the MBO process are identified and their relationships to the key managerial activities described earlier are also indicated.

An essential component of any MBO system is a set of well-formulated long-range goals and strategic plans for the organization (Step 1). These are generally based upon an analysis of the external environment and an assessment of organizational strengths and weaknesses. Inputs from the external environment generally take the form of opportunities or problems confronting the firm. Internal inputs, on the other hand, are primarily related to its technological, human, financial, physical, and other resources. Long-range goals and strategic plans provide a basis for determining current priorities and for establishing overall objectives for the organization and specific objectives for each subunit and its members (Steps 2, 3, and 4).

Clearly defined and verifiable objectives become the basis for more short-term action plans throughout the organization. These generally specify the details of *how* the objectives are to be achieved (Step 5). Up to this point, the emphasis is on planning as an intellectual or a "thinking" process. The implementation phase (Step 6) involves carrying out the activities specified in the action plans and, if and when required, taking corrective action. Periodic MBO reviews (Step 7) have a problem-solving focus and may result in a revision of goals, a change in action plans, or a modification of how the plans are implemented.

The periodic reviews also provide an important input into the evaluation of an individual's performance.

The individual performance review (Step 8) involves the appraisal of *overall* performance and in turn provides important inputs into several key activities. It helps to identify training and development needs (Step 8a) which are then translated into specific objectives that become part of the individual's job objectives for the next period. It also provides an important input into the amount of compensation he receives (Step 8b). It is important to note, however, that there are other variables besides current performance which determine his wages. Finally, the individual performance review provides the input needed for career and manpower planning (Step 8c). Individual career plans provide the basis for manpower planning, which is one of the internal inputs required to develop long-range goals and strategic plans, thus closing the loop in the system.

The potential advantages and disadvantages of applying MBO as an integrative system may not be obvious at this point. The concept can be no better than the way it is used. As we cover each aspect of the concept in greater detail, an attempt will be made to highlight both its benefits and its pitfalls.

THE LANGUAGE OF MBO

At this point there may be some confusion about the terms of MBO. What is the difference, for example, between a "goal" and an "objective"? a "target" and a "standard"? There seems to be little agreement in the literature. Some authors use the terms almost interchangeably. Others do not. For our purposes, however, it might be helpful to define them in a way which is consistent with the conceptual framework we are using.

A *goal* is a desired future condition. It reflects a statement of intent, something to shoot for. Its time-frame tends to be long-range, as distinguished from that of a short-term *target*, perhaps three to five years and longer. Goals tend to be broad in focus, though specific enough to provide direction and thrust. They may be expressed in either qualitative or quantitative terms. In management by objectives, however, the more specifically and concretely they are stated, the better. Some examples might include:

> "To increase profits to ten million dollars per year within five years."

"To increase commercial sales to 75% and decrease military sales to 25% by 1980."

"To establish a major division on the West Coast within three years and a major subsidiary in Eastern Europe within six years."

An *objective* is a desired accomplishment or hoped for result. It is a goal expressed in a specific dimension; it is narrower in focus; it has a shorter time-frame, perhaps six months to three years. As far as possible, objectives are expressed in quantitative, measurable, concrete terms, in the form of a written statement of desired results to be achieved within a given time period. For example:

"To increase our earnings per share to $2.50 this year."

"To introduce a new product in the $7.00–9.00 price range within two years."

"To decrease the monthly accident rate to 5% within six months."

A *target* is a specific desired result, or evidence of definite progress toward an objective. As such, its focus is very narrow compared to either objectives or goals. It is also very short-term. Targets are generally contained *within* an objective and contribute toward its attainment. They are generally expressed in precise, specific, and concrete terms:

"To introduce a new product in the $7.00–9.00 price range by March 15 and to sell 1000 units by December 31."

"To increase sales of product A to 850 units by March 1, product B to 465 units by July 1, and product C to 375 units by October 15."

A *standard of performance* is a description of the results of a job well done. It is specific, realistic, and feasible. It is also control-oriented. Standards of performance can be developed with regard to *all* of the elements of a given managerial job. They are usually expressed in the quantitative terms of "how much" and "by when":

"To meet 95% of all delivery dates scheduled this year."

"To maintain scrap loss at 3% per month over the next 18 months."

A *subjective* is used where an objective cannot be stated. It is generally established in areas where it is difficult to measure or confirm the actual attainment of an objective. Subjectives are expressed in terms of a number of specific *verifiable* activities or events which, when accomplished, should logically lead to the desired future state or condition:

> "To improve public relations with the community:
> (a) Publish and distribute a district-wide newsletter to all parent, teacher, and student groups each month.
> (b) Conduct 'open house' at least once a year at each school in the district.
> (c) Conduct weekly 'rap' sessions for student representatives in each intermediate and high school."
> "To improve communications in the plant:
> (a) Conduct weekly staff meetings with all department heads.
> (b) Publish a monthly employee newsletter beginning in March of this year.
> (c) Have lunch at least once a month with two or three randomly selected foremen."

Setting goals and objectives is perhaps the most critical element in the MBO process. Once their basic form and content have been determined, however, the problem of getting them down in writing becomes important. Objectives, especially, must be written in a way which clearly communicates their intent to all of the relevant parties. As indicated by the above, they must be expressed in tangible and measurable or verifiable terms. The language of MBO is clear and concise and does not permit ambiguity.

Some further examples

Poor: To improve our estimating procedures.
Better: To complete 95% of all production estimates for special sales inquiries within 48 working hours of receipt.

Poor: To improve teamwork in my department so as to increase the quality of work.
Better: To reduce the number of rejects to a maximum of 2% per month by the end of the current year without increasing budget.

Poor: To improve our profit picture.

Better: To obtain annual earnings after taxes within two years of (1) 12% on total assets, (2) 16% on shareholders' equity, and (3) 6% on sales.

Poor: To add a new product to our line.

Better: To introduce a new product in the *(specify)* price range by November 1 and to reach *x* number of units volume by May 1.

Poor: To be a socially responsible company.

Better: To hire and retain ten hard core unemployables within two years, and to promote two women to middle management positions by December 31.

Poor: To improve the reading ability of all students in our school.

Better: To increase the average reading scores of our students as follows: *(specify the average score or percentage increase for each grade level).*

Poor: To change the organization of my department.

Better: By July 1, to reorganize my department so as to accomplish 1, 2, and 3 *(itemize and specify).*

Poor: To conduct market research on product *x.*

Better: By July 1, to conduct market research which costs no more than $50,000 and will tell us 1, 2, and 3 *(specify)* about the product *x.*

Poor: To develop clearly defined work assignments so that I can assign any of my personnel to a number of different functions so as to develop their flexibility, maintain their interest, and expand their capabilities. Personnel will be rotated through these assignments monthly.

Better: To develop and conduct a job rotation training program that will assure that all personnel in my section can reasonably perform any work assignment. This is to be accomplished by August 1 and without an increase in my training budget.

Poor: To develop a plan to reduce idle employee time caused by the changeover of the production line.

Better: To develop and implement by September 1 a plan to reduce employee idle time during production line changeover by 50%, at a cost not to exceed $5000.

REFERENCES

Drucker, P. F. *The Practice of Management.* Harper & Row, 1954.

McGregor, D. M. "An uneasy look at performance appraisal." *Harvard Business Review* 35 (May-June 1957): 89–94.

McGregor, D. M. *The Human Side of Enterprise.* McGraw-Hill, 1960.

Schleh, E. C. *Management by Results.* McGraw-Hill, 1961.

Goals and Objectives

3

THE ROLE OF TOP MANAGEMENT

The importance of top management commitment to and participation in management by objectives has already been stressed. MBO will be limited to the Phase 1 and 2 programs described in the previous chapter if it does not have the firm support and active involvement of the chief executive and his top team. Top management's overriding responsibility for overall organizational planning has long been recognized by management theorists and practitioners alike. In an excellent and comprehensive treatment of the subject, Steiner (1969) makes the following observations:

1) Corporate planning will fail in the absence of the chief executive's support, participation, and guidance.
2) Corporate planning is the responsibility of the chief executive and cannot be delegated to a planning staff.
3) The chief executive is responsible for assuring that a proper organization for planning is created, that the manner of its functioning is clear and understood, and that it operates effectively and efficiently.
4) The chief executive must see that all managers understand that planning is a continuous function and not one pursued on an ad hoc basis or only during a formal planning cycle.

5) The chief executive should see that all managers recognize that planning means change, and the interaction of plans on people and institutions must be understood and considered.

6) Once plans are prepared, top management must make decisions on the basis of plans.

Someone long ago said that the best fertilizer ever invented was the footsteps of the farmer. Similarly, the best assurance of effective planning in an organization is the active participation of the chief executive in doing it.

It is essential, then, that the chief executive and his top team provide the direction and thrust for the MBO system. They must become actively involved in formulating long-range goals and strategic plans, in providing the mechanisms for their implementation, and in developing the specific short-range performance objectives for the organization. These inputs are essential to any integrative MBO system. Perhaps equally as important, however, they help communicate to all members of the organization the level and depth of top management commitment to the philosophy, method, and process of managing by and with objectives.

A cascade approach

As sketched in Figure 3–1, individual managerial objectives are generally derived from organizational goals and objectives which tend to "cascade" down through the organizational hierarchy in the following manner:

1) The process begins at the top with a clear, concise statement of the central purpose of the enterprise.

2) Long-range organizational goals and the strategic plans for their attainment are formulated from this statement.

3) These in turn lead to the establishment of more short-range performance objectives for the organization. When tied to a specified time period such as a year, overall organizational performance objectives become the basis for and an integral part of the objectives of the chief executive and his top management team.

4) Derivative objectives are then developed for each major

FIGURE 3–1. A Cascade Approach to Goal Setting.

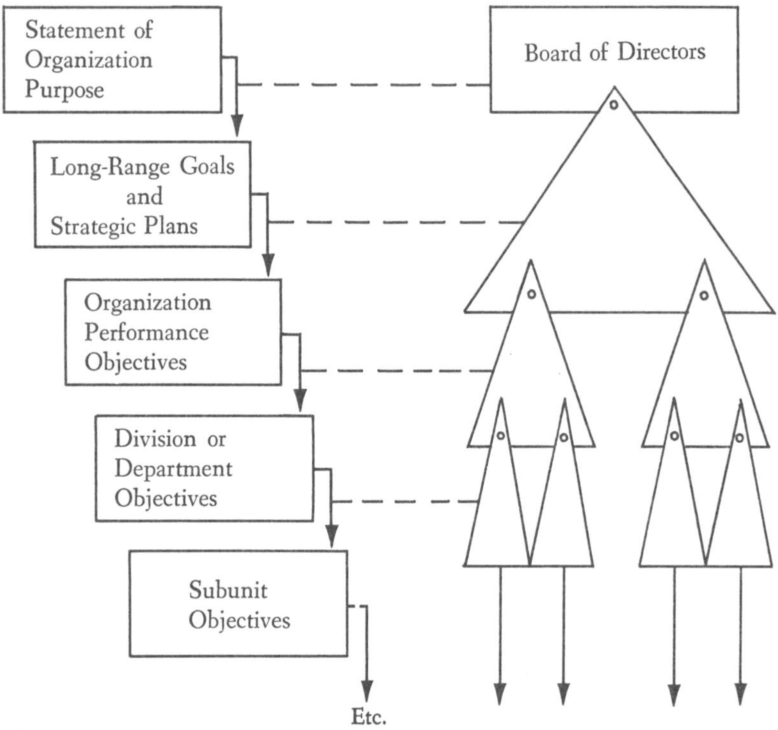

division or department. These, in turn, provide important inputs into the MBO system at that level of management.

5) Objectives are then established for the various subunits in each major division or department. As above, subunit objectives provide the basis for managing by objectives at that given level.

6) And so on down through the organizational hierarchy.

It should not be assumed that the cascade approach to goal setting involves autocratic or "top down" management. Nothing could be further from the truth. The successful implementation of an MBO system requires a great deal of involvement and participation in the

goal-setting process on the part of managers at all levels of the organization. Drucker (1954) describes the process as follows:

> The goals of each manager's job must be defined by the con-
> tribution he has to make to the success of the larger unit of
> which he is a part. The objectives of the district sales manager's
> job should be defined by the contribution he and his district
> sales force have to make to the sales department, the objectives
> of the project engineer's job by the contribution he, his engi-
> neers and draftsmen make to the engineering department. . . .
>
> This requires each manager to develop and set the objectives
> of his unit himself. Higher management must of course reserve
> the power to approve or disapprove these objectives. But their
> development is part of a manager's responsibility; indeed, it is
> his first responsibility. It means, too, that every manager should
> responsibly participate in the development of the objectives of
> the higher unit of which he is a part. . . . Precisely because
> his aim should reflect the objective needs of the business,
> rather than merely what the individual manager wants, he
> must commit himself to them with a positive act of assent. He
> must know and understand the ultimate business goals, what
> is expected of him and why, what he will be measured against
> and how. There must be a 'meeting of the minds' within the
> entire management of each unit. This can be achieved only
> when each of the contributing managers is expected to think
> through what the unit objectives are, is led, in other words, to
> participate actively and responsibly in the work of defining
> them. And only if his lower managers participate in this way
> can the higher manager know what to expect of them and
> make exacting demands.

The statement of organizational purpose

As indicated earlier, a clear and concise statement of purpose
or mission is an important frame of reference for most organizational
activities. It is particularly important to a system of management by
objectives. It provides the basis for the formulation of long-range goals
and strategic plans; it serves to focus management's attention on common needs; it helps to identify and define key areas of organizational

performance and activity; and it provides a basis for judging the potential value of short-term actions.

The definition of organizational purpose requires answering a number of fundamental questions: "Why does this organization exist?" "What is the present scope of the enterprise?" "What is its potential?" Turning such basic questions into a well-phrased statement of purpose can have a profound impact on the success or failure of the enterprise. Consider, for example, the radical change in mission made by the Cunard Line in 1966. In the words of Cunard's chairman of the board: "If we regard the passenger ship no longer simply as a means of transport, but more as a floating resort in which people take a holiday and enjoy themselves, and incidentally get transportation thrown in, then the market outlook is completely changed. We find ourselves in a growth industry, the leisure industry" (*Fortune,* January 1967, p. 58).

The business firm's top management must define its mission practically, by using its best thinking to produce some statement that sufficiently answers some of the key questions in a number of relevant areas:

The business entity • What is our present business? What should it be? What kinds of business in terms of products, markets, resources, size, etc., are required to satisfy our need for growth?

The markets • Who are our present customers? How well do we meet their needs? What unsatisfied needs must we be prepared to meet? What new markets offer us the best potential for growth?

The overall strategy • What is our present master strategy? What distinct capabilities do we possess? How are we unique in the industry? What niche do we now hold? What can it be in the future? What are some of the possible significant moves that might be made by our competitors that could affect our present and future position? How durable is our present strategy? What changes appear to be needed?

The internal organization • Does our present structure and environment facilitate effective collaboration throughout the organization? Are problem-solving and decision-making consistent with the deployment of our resources? Does our organizational climate support other key areas of concern such as human satisfaction? What internal changes can we make, in terms of both structure and processes, that would facilitate our growth and development?

The investors • What is our present return on investment? How acceptable is it? How does this compare with the rest of the industry? What kind of growth rate do we desire? Are our present policies and practices consistent with the needs of our investors?

The society • What contributions do we presently make to the community at large? How will societal needs and demands affect our company over the next five years or so? What is our commitment as a member of society? What changes do we want to make in terms of fulfilling our responsibility to society at large?

Defining (or redefining) the basic mission of the organization in a well-phrased statement of purpose provides a solid foundation upon which to build a more effective system of managing by objectives.

LONG-RANGE GOALS AND STRATEGIC PLANS

Defining its purpose provides an organization with a clear sense of its basic mission and sets the stage for strategic planning, but formulating long-range goals and strategic plans is the first major step in the MBO process (see Figure 3–2). This is essentially a process of establishing the major long-run goals of the organization and specifying the

FIGURE 3–2.   MBO as a System: Step 1.

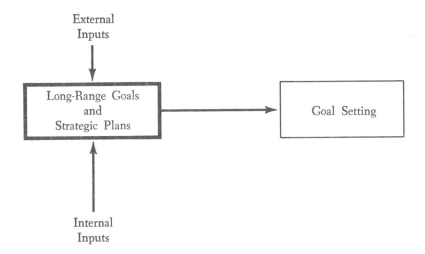

FIGURE 3–3. The Process of Strategic Planning.

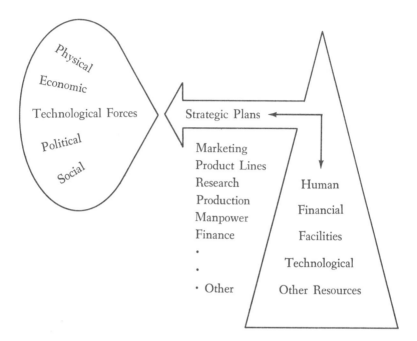

• Analyze External Environment   • Assess Organizational Capabilities

way in which resources will be deployed to achieve them. Strategic plans generally reflect the means for survival and growth; that is, they describe how the organization plans to cope with its total environment.

The content or subject matter of strategic planning may conceivably include every type of relevant activity. For the business firm, for example, these include profits, pricing, marketing, finance, public relations, capital budgeting, personnel, production, management selection and development, legal and political activities, and many others.

Although strategic plans are generally more long-term, they may cover different time periods for different subjects or activities. For example, a strategic plan to acquire another company may be formulated and implemented within a relatively short time period to take advantage of a rare opportunity.

A simplified version of the strategic planning process is illustrated in Figure 3–3. It can be seen that the formulation of strategic plans involves two major elements: the analysis of the external environment and an assessment of the organization's internal resources. Each in turn involves a number of other factors and considerations.

Analyzing the external environment

The external environment generally includes those factors which affect the organization's success or failure. Although they may be subject to long-term fluctuations, they are forces which management can neither order nor control. They include such things as general economic trends, government policies and regulations, the actions of competitors, technological advancements, and sociopolitical changes.

The continuous and ongoing analysis of these external factors is essential to the survival and prosperity of business firms. To begin with, existing product lines must be systematically analyzed. Management must find new opportunities for present products, new applications, customers, or locations; it must search for new opportunities to serve existing customers with new products or new applications; it must identify present and future threats to the company's market position and profit margins. The analysis might be guided by such relevant questions in key areas as:

The markets • What are the major problems or threats to our existing markets and product lines? What are the opportunities?

The product lines • What are the supply and demand characteristics of our major products or product groups? What are their price characteristics? What do their life cycles look like? At what stages are they?

The customers • What are some of the trends or changes in terms of customer needs? What are some of the inherent risks we face in meeting these needs?

Potential substitutes • What is the possibility that substitute products or services will emerge? How likely is this to happen? When?

The analysis can then be expanded to include a search for opportunities for new products and product lines. This frequently involves a search for new markets and new customers. It may also include an analysis of the activities of competitors, especially in the development of new products of their own. Some guiding questions might include:

New products • In what areas are there opportunities for new products? What is their potential? What are some of the present needs of consumers that are not yet being met? What are some of the anticipated future needs? What are our competitors doing in terms of new product development?

A critical analysis of the external environment is a necessary element in the strategic planning process. It involves the systematic, continuous assessment of the problems, opportunities, and risks confronting the enterprise, all of which must be considered if the organization is to prosper and grow in its total environment.

Assessing organizational capabilities

Although forces in the external environment affect the design of strategic plans, the availability of internal resources is generally the limiting factor. The assessment of organizational capabilities, then, involves a realistic evaluation of *both* its strengths *and* its weaknesses. It provides the basis for developing strategic alternatives in the light of what the organization can *actually* do to assure its continued growth and success. The key analytical questions generally center around four different types of internal resources:

Technical resources • What is the current state of our technology? What is its potential? How do they compare to the rest of the industry? How might we best meet the technological challenges of the future?

Physical resources • What is the present condition of our plant and equipment? How flexible are they? How do our operating costs compare with those of our competitors? What is our break-even point? How well do we utilize our potential capacity? To what other uses can we economically put our physical resources?

Financial resources • What is our return on investment and our pattern of earnings? What is our present financial condition? What is our ability to generate cash? What is our present capital structure? What is the availability of both short- and long-term credit? If and when needed, how accessible is new equity capital? How do our financial resources compare with those of our competitors?

Human resources • Do we have the technical skills we presently need in all areas? What is our future potential? How does it compare with the rest of the industry? Do we presently have the necessary management skills at all levels? What is the future potential of our management team? How does it compare to that of other organizations? What is the attitude of our total work force? What changes do we need to make to be more effective now and in the future?

The assessment of organizational capabilities also involves an orderly and continuous review of markets, products, processes, reputation, and position in the industry vis à vis customers, competitors, relevant government agencies, suppliers, and others.

Developing strategic plans

The development of sound strategic plans, then, is based upon a systematic analysis of the relevant forces in the external environment and a realistic assessment of internal resources. It is fundamentally a problem of matching and integrating what an organization *can* do with what it *might* do.

Perhaps it should be noted at this time, however, that the decisions which go into the process are not based solely on economics and rationality. The analysis, the assessment, the evaluations, and the interpretations are all influenced by the personal values, the aspirations, and the sense of social responsibility held by top management. The human notions of what they "want to do" and "should do" are an important influence in the strategic planning process. They help shape the final product.

There are a number of elements that add body and substance to strategic plans. Assuming that a clear statement and understanding of the organization's mission already exists, a sound strategic plan might include all or most of the following: a specified goal or set of goals; a description of major activities and key events; a logical sequencing of activities; a timetable or projected time-lines; a procedure for measuring and reviewing progress; and supporting budgets, financial plans, and manpower tables.

SPECIFIC ORGANIZATIONAL GOALS

As indicated in Figure 3–4, this is the second major step in the MBO process. It is one of the essential activities required to translate long-range goals and strategic plans into action. To become operational, however, they must be specific and their attainment capable of being

FIGURE 3–4.   MBO as a System: Steps 2 and 3.

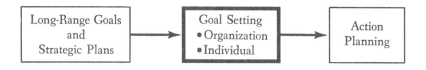

measured. Objectives couched in vague platitudes are of little value to the organization or to its members. For example, a set of objectives which includes "to maximize profits and return on investment," "to develop new and high-quality products," and "to meet our corporate social responsibility" provides little or no direction to management efforts. How much profit is desired? When? What kinds of new products are to be developed? Quality at what cost? What kinds of public activities? To what extent? If organizational objectives are to provide the backbone for an effective system of managing by objectives, they must be concrete and verifiable. That is, management must be able to respond to the fundamental question, "How will you know when they have been attained?"

The overall objectives should specify the performance, activities, and results to be accomplished by the organization as a whole within a given time span. They cover both the economic and noneconomic areas of the enterprise. The setting of specific objectives in a business organization might follow the pattern described below, and is based upon the identification of *key result areas*.

The key areas of performance and results consist of those activities which are vital to the success of the enterprise. Numerous lists of these areas have been developed over the past two decades or so, but they show fewer differences than similarities. The following list is a comprehensive summary of the literature and illustrates the nature of specific objectives in these key areas.

1) *Profitability* can be expressed in terms of profits, return on investment, earnings per share, or profit-to-sales ratios, among others. Objectives in this area may be expressed in such concrete and specific terms as "to increase return on investment to 15 percent after taxes within five years" or "to increase profits to six million dollars next year."

2) *Markets* may also be described in a number of different ways, including share of the market, dollar or unit volume of sales, and niche in the industry. To illustrate, marketing objectives might be "to increase share of market to 28 percent within three years," "to sell 200,000 units next year," or "to increase commercial sales to 85 percent and reduce military sales to 15 percent over the next two years."

3) *Productivity* objectives may be expressed in terms of ratio of input to output (e.g., "To increase number of units to x amount per worker per eight-hour day"). The objectives may also be expressed in terms of cost per unit of production.

4) *Product* objectives, aside from sales and profitability by product or product line, may be stated as, for example, "to introduce a product in the middle range of our product line within two years" or "to phase out the rubber products by the end of next year."

5) *Financial resource* objectives may be expressed in many different ways, depending upon the company, such as capital structure, new issues of common stock, cash flow, working capital, dividend payments, and collection periods. Some illustrations include "to decrease the collection period to 26 days by the end of the year," "to increase working capital to five million dollars within three years," and "to reduce long-term debt to eight million dollars within five years."

6) *Physical facilities* may be described in terms of square feet, fixed cost, units of production, and many other measurements. Objectives might be "to increase production capacity to 8 million units per month within two years" or "to increase storage capacity to 15 million barrels next year."

7) *Research and innovation* objectives may be expressed in dollars as well as in other terms: "to develop an engine in the (*specify*) price range, with an emission rate of less than 10 percent, within two years at a cost not to exceed $150,000."

8) *Organization*—changes in structure or activities are also included and may be expressed in any number of ways, such as "to design and implement a matrix organizational structure within two years" or "to establish a regional office in the South by the end of next year."

9) *Human resource* objectives may be quantitatively expressed in terms of absenteeism, tardiness, number of griev-

ances, and training, such as "to reduce absenteeism to less than 4 percent by the end of next year" or "to conduct a twenty-hour in-house management training program for 120 front-line supervisors by the end of 1975 at a cost not to exceed $200 per participant."

10) *Social responsibility* objectives may be expressed in terms of types of activities, number of days of service, or financial contributions. An example might be "to hire 120 hard-core unemployables within the next two years."

The above list is by no means exhaustive and is intended only to illustrate the various areas and ways in which specific objectives can be established for the overall organization. Although the focus is on the business firm, the same process and guidelines may be applied to other types of organizations as well.

DEPARTMENTAL OBJECTIVES

Step 3 in the MBO process involves developing precise derivative objectives for the major divisions, departments, and subunits, though the degree of precision, like the process itself, must be tailored for each organization. There are even differences *within* the same organization in terms of the nature of available data, the degree to which objectives can be quantified, the number of levels of management involved in MBO, and many other variables. The following four substeps illustrate how derivative objectives might be established at various levels of the organization with an increasing degree of precision and quantification.

Divide each key result area into subareas

These subareas may be identified as those centers of activity in which a relatively small number of events yield a relatively high percentage of the results. Improvement in the key result area is assured when management does a good job in these areas. The key result area "marketing," for example, may be further divided into sales volume, share of market, market penetration, and customer acceptance, though the relative degree of importance of each subarea is subject to changes in the firm's situation.

Assign derivative objectives to divisions or departments

The next step involves developing derivative objectives in the major subareas and assigning them to the appropriate division or departments. These may be further broken down for assignment to lower-level subunits. Of the subareas identified in the preceding step, for example, *sales volume* and *market penetration* might be further broken down by product and assigned to regions, to districts, and eventually even to the individual salesmen, while *share of market* and *customer acceptance* might also be developed for each product and be further defined in terms of national and foreign marketplaces. Depending upon the availability of data, however, the latter two would probably remain at the divisional level.

Develop and specify measures and standards

Measures and standards may then be developed for each key result area and its related subareas. (Measures are essentially criteria which can be used to determine acceptable standards, as defined in Chapter 2.) In a few instances, the level of past performance may be carried forward, but in many areas and subareas standards can be significantly increased. Following are some illustrations of measures and standards for the subareas listed in Step 3a above:

1) Sales volume measured by total dollar revenues for the year, with a standard of 50 million dollars.

2) Share of market measured by percentage of total dollar volume of industry sales, with a standard of 15%.

3) Market penetration measured by percentage increase in the number of sales outlets, with a standard of 5% per quarter.

4) Customer acceptance measured by new customer sales volume as a percentage of total sales, with a standard of 6% per year.

Establish an improvement target and date

A target generally reflects the degree of improvement desired beyond a standard. It should reflect a realistic challenge and should be attainable within a reasonable period of time. Examples of how improvement targets and dates might be established for three of the objectives developed above are:

1) To increase *sales volume* by ten million dollars over a 50 million dollar standard, for a total of 60 million dollars, by the end of 1975.

2) To increase the *share of market* by 3% over a 15% standard, for a total of 18% of industry sales, by the second quarter of 1975.

3) To increase *market penetration* by 1% over a 5% per quarter standard, for a 6% increase in the number of outlets, by the third quarter of 1975.

It is obvious that all of the objectives and derivative objectives in each key result area cannot be as precisely defined, measured, standardized, and targeted for improvement as those illustrated above. Many objectives in a number of key result areas may be extremely difficult, if not impossible, to quantify. In some instances the required data may simply not be available. It is suggested that "subjectives" be used in these difficult and more qualitative areas.

ILLUSTRATION

Following is a simplified illustration which attempts to relate the cascade approach to goal-setting and the first three major steps in the MBO process:

Step 1: Formulate long-range goals and strategic plans

The goal: To increase return on investment to 15% after taxes by the end of five years (*specify percentage for each year*).
The strategic plan: (1) To increase share of market through

greater market penetration and the introduction of a medium-priced product; and (2) to reduce average cost per unit to increase competitive advantage.

Step 2: Develop specific organizational goals

1) Increase sales volume to 100,000 units next year.
   a. Increase product A to 70,000 units.
   b. Increase product B to 30,000 units.
2) Expand existing production facilities to produce 100,000 units at no additional cost per unit next year.
3) Reduce manufacturing cost per unit on existing products by 10% next year.
4) Construct additional modern facilities to produce 50,000 units in two years.
5) Develop a new product in the (specify) price range within two years at a cost not to exceed $150,000.
6) Reduce long-term debt to 8 million dollars within two years.
7) Recruit and train 22 semiskilled workers next year.

Step 3: Establish departmental objectives

Marketing Department

1) Increase sales volume to 100,000 units next year (specify by product).
   a. Increase eastern region sales to 35,000 units (specify by product).
      (1) Increase New York district sales to (specify by number of units per product).
      (2) Increase New England district sales to (specify by number of units per product).
      (3) Increase other district sales to (specify by number of units per product).
   b. Increase midwestern region sales to 20,000 units (specify by product).

  c. Increase southern region sales to 15,000 units (*specify by product*).

  d. Increase western region sales to 30,000 units (*specify by product*).

 2) Increase share of market to 17% next year.

Production Department

 1) Expand existing facilities to produce 100,000 units next year.

  a. Improve production scheduling.

  b. Increase work force by 22 workers.

 2) Reduce manufacturing costs per unit on existing products at no increase in cost per unit next year.

  a. Reduce scrap by 10% next year.

  b. Reduce inventories by 15% next year.

Engineering Department

 1) Construct and equip by (*date*) a modern plant capable of producing 50,000 units efficiently.

  a. Approved building and equipment plans by (*date*).

  b. Complete construction by (*date*).

  c. Install and test equipment by (*date*).

R&D Department

 1) Develop a new product in the (*specify*) price range within two years at a cost not to exceed $150,000.

  a. Complete prototype by (*date*).

  b. Complete testing by (*date*).

Finance Department

 1) Reduce long-term debt to 8 million dollars within two years.

  a. Reduce long-term debt to 9 million dollars next year.

  b. Decrease average collection period to 21 days.

  c. Increase working capital to $750,000 next year.

Personnel Department

 1) Recruit and train 22 semiskilled workers next year.

  a. Recruit and select 22 assemblers by (*date*).

b. Design and develop training program by (*date*).
c. Conduct and complete training by (*date*).

REFERENCES

Drucker, P. F. *The Practice of Management.* Harper & Row, 1954, pp. 128–29.
Steiner, G. A. *Top Management Planning.* Macmillan, 1969, pp. 103–4.

Individual Job Objectives

4

THE NATURE OF JOB OBJECTIVES

The process of managing by objectives requires a high degree of participation and collaboration among members of the organization. This generally involves the identification of common goals and objectives and the coordination of individual and group efforts toward achieving them. The emphasis is primarily on the future, on change for the better, on where the organization is going, and on how it intends to get there. One purpose of this fourth step in the MBO process (see Figure 4-1) is to distill specific individual job objectives from organizational goals and plans, while at the same time seeing to it that they are appropriately assigned and linked to each other at all levels of the enterprise. Organizational objectives determine the priorities and key activities of organizational units and subunits. A set of job objectives for an individual manager, on the other hand, determines the nature and scope of his work activities. In this regard, they supplement his job description. Once objectives have been formulated and assumed by organizational units and individuals, they become the basis for the activities and performance required for their attainment. Continuous attention is then paid to such things as the methods of achieving the objectives, the use of required resources, timing, interactions with other members, and the appraisal of performance.

FIGURE 4–1.   MBO as a System: Step 4.

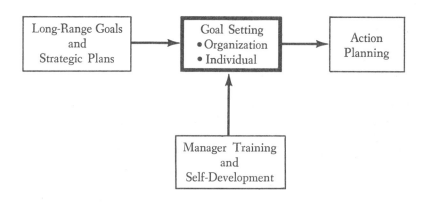

The involvement of individual managers (or nonmanagers for that matter) in setting objectives for their own jobs can result in a number of significant benefits and changes for all concerned. To begin with, the individual develops a greater awareness of his managerial role in the organization. He becomes more conscious of overall goals and objectives. The better he understands them, the more accurately he can develop his own role and the part he plays in their attainment and the more able he is to develop meaningful objectives in his area of responsibility. This suggests a high level of participation, or at least some involvement, in the process of setting the objectives of his organizational unit. Vertical and horizontal work relationships are also improved. The necessity for more contact and communication tends to break down protective barriers and provides the basis for realistic, clear-cut accountability for results. Perhaps most important, the individual develops a new level of motivation and sense of accomplishment. The achievement of self-formulated objectives can become an important motivating factor to improve job performance.

Given the complexity of most managerial positions, however, it would be virtually impossible to develop job objectives which cover each and every area of responsibility for a given individual. Consequently, the emphasis should be on those segments or activities which relate to one or more of the key result areas of a given job. The major job segments for a production manager, for example, might include production scheduling and delivery, the quality of the product, and operating efficiency. The key activities of a sales manager might include sales forecasting, customer service, and sales contacts in the field.

Managerial job objectives may be further divided into those which deal with an individual's *performance* and those which deal with his *personal development*. Performance objectives relate primarily to the manager's job or position assignment, while personal development objectives relate to his skill and potential. It should be noted at this point that performance objectives may be further distinguished in terms of those which are aimed at *maintaining* a given level of performance and those which are aimed at *improving* the performance level. Maintenance objectives are most useful in MBO when they serve to maintain desired standards of performance. They are generally related to the routine and repetitive aspects of an individual's job and are usually expressed in absolute terms. Improvement objectives, on the other hand, are usually expressed as relative changes. Given the focus on improvement and change, improvement objectives tend to be dominant in most MBO systems.

Performance objectives

Performance objectives are derived directly from the job assignment. Though they may take the form of special activities or projects which are not normally part of the job, but instead arise from emergencies, changes in priorities, or other management decisions, they are invariably directly related to the areas of responsibility and the activities managed by the individual. Performance objectives may be further categorized as follows:

Routine activities in key result areas • Every managerial position includes a variety of ongoing, repetitive activities which must be accomplished. A plant manager, for example, prepares production schedules, maintains inventories, meets scheduled delivery dates, controls waste and spoilage, and prepares work assignments. The existence and development of standards of performance in key result areas is central to setting routine job objectives. Those which are maintenance-oriented essentially reflect acceptable standards of performance. Improvement objectives, on the other hand, are generally based upon targets which reflect changes in those standards. The process usually involves developing standards of performance in selected key result areas of the job, and establishing objectives and targets which are expressed as improvements over the standards. Maintenance objectives may then be established in those areas not selected for improvement to ensure that overall performance does not decrease.

To carry our illustration further, let us assume that acceptable standards of performance for our plant manager in two of his key result areas are: "a 95% on-time delivery rate for scheduled deliveries," and "a 5% spoilage and waste factor." Maintenance objectives in these areas for the year might be expressed as follows:

"To meet 95% of all scheduled delivery dates."

"To limit spoilage and waste to 5% of all raw materials used."

On the other hand, after a careful analysis and discussions with his boss, he may decide to improve his performance in these two areas. Expressed as improvement objectives, his statements might read as follows:

"To increase deliveries to 98% of all scheduled delivery dates."

"To reduce spoilage and waste to 3% of all raw materials used."

Special activities • There are also a number of special activities, assignments, and projects that from time to time become part of the managerial job. These may result from emergencies, special projects, changes in priorities, or may simply result from management decisions. For example, our plant manager may be informed by the personnel department that 290 man-days of labor were lost the previous year as a result of accidents in the plant. He has been asked by his boss to investigate the causes and to reduce lost time due to in-plant accidents to an "acceptable" level. He has also been asked to reduce his operating cost as part of a company-wide economy drive. His set of job objectives for the year, then, might also include the following statements:

"To reduce lost time due to accidents in the plant to 100 man-days per year," and

"To reduce operating cost to 10% below budget."

Innovative and creative activities • The greatest potential for improvement lies in the solution of persistent problems and the introduction of new ideas for achieving better results. Consequently, no small part of the manager's activities should be aimed at innovating, at creating new methods, and at introducing changes which improve individual and organizational performance. Creativity and innovation in MBO can be sparked in a number of different ways. Odiorne distinguishes between "extrinsic" creativity, which results from the introduction of new ideas from the outside, and "intrinsic" creativity, which results from the discovery of new ways or methods of doing the present job (Odiorne, 1965). Our plant manager, for example, may have been struggling with a less than adequate quality control system for the past several years. Because of his healthy curiosity about new developments in manufacturing, he learns about a new quality control technique which utilizes radioisotopes. He conducts a feasibility study to determine whether or not the new technique could be used in his plant. In addition to the quality control problem, though, he has been considering ways to increase the overall utilization time of the special-purpose machinery on the production line. The following statements might be included among his creative objectives:

> "To install a radioisotope system of quality control this year at a cost not to exceed $53,000" (extrinsic creativity).
>
> "To improve production scheduling and preventative maintenance techniques so as to increase machine utilization time to 95 percent of capacity without increasing maintenance cost" (intrinsic creativity).

Personal development objectives

The establishment of personal development objectives hardly implies that there is no learning or training inherent in the pursuit and achievement of performance objectives. The opposite is in fact true. Job objectives that focus on improvement actually contribute a great deal to a manager's growth and development. Beyond this, however, there are personal needs and skills that can have a significant impact on his present motivation and his future potential.

Personal development objectives may be established for any of several reasons. To begin with, they may be aimed at improving technical competence. This is especially important in high technology organizations. They can also be aimed at increasing managerial skills. There are numerous potential benefits to be derived from additional training in management methods and techniques. Objectives in both these areas may be aimed at improving present performance or preparing the individual for advancement. New or additional technical or managerial skills may be required for higher-level positions.

The inclusion of personal objectives provides a unique opportunity to integrate individual needs with organizational goals. The manager is likely to have a higher level of motivation and sense of commitment to the *total* set of job objectives when he has a personal stake in them. The essence of personal development objectives, then, lies in their potential to improve current performance, to combat technological and managerial obsolescence, to prepare the individual for additional responsibility and advancement, and to increase his level of motivation and commitment to his total set of job objectives.

There is an almost unlimited number of objectives and activities which can contribute to individual growth and development. Odiorne (1965, p. 137) offers some two dozen illustrations, including taking and teaching courses in local institutions or the company, organizational and community service work, continuing education, writing professional papers, and improving (with medical advice) personal health. The number and extent of personal development objectives formulated for a given time period, however, will vary from individual to individual and from organization to organization. A working line manager, for example, probably would include only two or three of them among his job objectives. A young trainee might include a few more. High technology organizations generally place considerably more emphasis on the problem of technological obsolescence than do organizations engaged in routine manufacturing activities. In the case of our plant manager, therefore, the following personal development objectives might be formulated for the goal-setting period:

> "To attend and successfully complete the UCLA Executive Program."
>
> "To teach a production management course in the University Extension evening program."

THE PROCESS OF SETTING JOB OBJECTIVES

It may be helpful at this point to restate some of the assumptions underlying the development of individual managerial objectives in an MBO system. First of all, it is assumed that overall organizational goals and objectives for the given period have been established and made known. Second, it is assumed that the objectives of higher levels of management have been established and communicated to the lower levels. And finally, it is assumed that as far as possible all organizational goals and objectives have been expressed in measurable, tangible, or verifiable terms.

The process we are about to describe is neither new nor original. It is equally appropriate for all levels of management and can be used for either line or staff positions, as well as nonmanagers. Given the philosophy of participation which underlies management by objectives, the quality of the interaction between the individual manager and other relevant members of the organization is critical to the success of the process. Our experience indicates that setting managerial job objectives tends to be most successful when the individual himself assumes responsibility for initiating the process and interacting with others, especially his supervisors, in a creative and problem-solving manner. This generally includes a series of sequential but interrelated steps which involve:

1) identifying the key functions and activities of the job;
2) assigning priorities or rankings to them;
3) developing acceptable standards of performance for these selected areas;
4) establishing improvement objectives, with targets and dates where appropriate;
5) communicating and modifying the objectives prior to implementation and subsequent review.

Step 1: Identify key functions and activities

Every managerial position should contain job functions and activities which directly relate to one or more of the organization's key result areas. As indicated earlier, these may be further classified as being routine, special, or creative in nature. For the time being we will ignore those which are concerned with the personal development of the individual. The manager's first task, then, is to identify a limited number of key functions or activities which offer a high potential for improved performance. He must consider those functions and activities for which the greatest benefits can be realized with a minimum expenditure of time and resources. He must consider those areas which, if improved, will remove bottlenecks and obstacles. And he must relate them to higher-level management objectives as well as the overall goals and strategies of the enterprise. The following questions may help to guide his analysis:

> 1) Which organizational goals and higher-level management objectives require my support?
> 2) What specific functions, tasks, and activities of mine provide this support?
> 3) What is my current level of performance in these areas?
> 4) What tangible data do I have to measure results in these areas and how reliable are they?
> 5) Which key functions and activities offer the highest potential for increasing my contribution to organizational goals and higher-level objectives?
> 6) How can the maximum benefit be realized with a minimum of cost?
> 7) What will be the impact of improved results in these areas on other managers and organizational units?

Step 2: Assign priorities or relative weights

The next step in the process involves assigning some sort of priority or relative weighting to each of the selected key functions and activities. Depending upon their nature and the relationship between them, this may be accomplished in several different ways. The objectives may be simply ranked in order of importance, with the most important one ranked first, the next most important second, and so on down the line. Activities based upon integrated job segments, on the other hand, lend themselves more readily to a system of weights of some sort, as follows:

Objective	Relative Weight
#1	35%
#2	25%
#3	15%
#4	10%
#5	7%
#6	5%
#7	3%
	100%

Other methods involve assigning each objective to a predefined and coded category of importance. Special activities and projects, for example, are more adaptable to an "A–B–C" priority system similar to the one presented below:

Priority Code		Description
A	=	"Must do" objectives *critical* to successful performance. They may be the result of special demands from higher levels of management or other external sources.
B	=	"Should do" objectives *necessary* for improved performance. They are generally vital, but their achievement can be postponed if necessary.
C	=	"Nice to do" objectives *desirable* for improved performance, but not critical to survival or improved performance. They can be eliminated or postponed to achieve objectives of higher priority.

A relative weighting system is generally more suitable for routine objectives and an "A–B–C" system is generally more suitable for assigning priorities to special project and innovative objectives. The following checklist may be of some use in helping to keep the priorities and relative weights in their proper focus:

1) Distinguish between the "must do," "should do," and "nice to do."

2) Focus on contributions to organizational goals and higher-level management objectives.

3) Concentrate on activities and results that will make a real difference rather than on things that are safe and easy to do.

4) Emphasize opportunities for improvement and de-emphasize problems to be solved.

5) Adhere to priorities by plan rather than to priorities by pressure.

6) Apply disciplined priority analysis and avoid climbing on the bandwagon.

7) Reassign priorities periodically to keep up with change and progress.

As the manager goes through a systematic analysis of priorities, he is also developing some decision-making guidelines which will help him in the future. He will know, for example, how maximum gains can be attained within a minimum time-frame; how more benefits can be gained with less cost; how to delegate and assign tasks better; how to allocate organization resources more effectively; how to modify policies, procedures, and work methods so as to yield the best results; how to monitor and control work activities strategically; and how to take corrective action whenever necessary.

Step 3: Develop standards of performance

Earlier a standard of performance was defined as a quantitative description of a job well done. The whole idea of accountability in management is based upon measurable standards which involve such factors as quantity, quality, cost, and time. A standard is generally derived from past levels of satisfactory or acceptable performance and, as long as the measurement factor remains constant, provides the basis for setting objectives and targets for the future.

A good illustration of the use of performance standards and measurable results can be found in professional baseball. A player's performance as a batter is generally measured by the percentage of hits he gets in total times at bat during the scheduled season. In three consecutive seasons he may compile a batting average of .306. He becomes known as a ".300 hitter," which is a performance standard. Other important standards for him can be established in "runs batted in," "runs scored," and several other categories. His objective for the coming season might be to hit for an average of .320 and to improve his performance in some of the other categories.

The third step in the process, then, involves the development of standards of performance for each of the identified key functions and activities. These in turn become the basis upon which to set objectives and to measure performance. A number of useful guidelines have been formulated to assist in the establishment of well-defined standards of managerial performance:

1) Standards should be defined by each individual for his own managerial position with the advice and counsel of his supervisor.

2) Standards should specify the required results on which satisfactory performance will be based.

3) Standards should include tangible measures which determine the performance of tasks with reasonable accuracy and reliability.

4) The measures of standards and results should be written clearly and concisely to prevent ambiguity.

5) Standards should provide for consistent evaluation and control of the quantity, quality, cost, and time factors of performance.

6) The format for documenting standards should facilitate goal setting and performance evaluation.

7) Standards of performance should be determined for all jobs which contribute to key result areas of the organization.

8) Standards should be revised to fit the realities of changing requirements, conditions, resources, capabilities, and competences.

When there is a lack of standards of performance in a managerial job, there is no "score card" on which to note progress. Perhaps equally as important, however, there is no factual basis for accountability. Accountability then becomes a matter of guesswork, opinions, attitudes, personal attributes, and feelings. A key to developing and expanding the managerial role in MBO lies in accountability derived from reliable measures of results, proven standards of performance, and systematic performance appraisal and reporting.

Before we leave the question of standards, however, it should be repeated that there are some aspects of the managerial job which do not lend themselves to measurement or quantification. This is especially true for new projects and special assignments. It is nevertheless important that an attempt be made to focus on activities and results that can be measured or at least verified by the relevant parties. At worst, the manager can resort to the use of "subjectives."

Step 4: Establish objectives

Setting objectives and subobjectives for the coming period is the most critical step in the process. An objective has been defined as a desired state or accomplishment, a specified and desired result to be accomplished within a given period of time. It represents progress, a gain beyond past accomplishments, a tangible improvement over existing conditions. Objectives must be set for each of the key areas identified in Step 1, though subjectives may be used when objectives cannot be quantified or formulated in measurable terms.

A number of criteria can be applied to objectives to help determine their nature and scope and to assist in their formulation. A meaningful management objective should reflect the following characteristics:

Challenging • The objective should present a challenge to the man. It should make him "stretch." How difficult is it to achieve the objective? How much cushion is there? How much incentive is there to apply unused potential? What is the likelihood of failure to reach the objective? What would be the cost of failure?

Attainable • On the other hand, the objective should be both realistic and achievable. How great is the risk? What support is needed? Is that support available? What is new and different to the operation? What changes would be involved? What is needed in the way of additional resources? At what cost?

Measurable • The objective should be as specific and quantitative as possible. It should be expressed in tangible and measurable terms. If it is a subjective, the results of its achievement should be verifiable. What data are needed to measure or verify the results? In what form? And at what intervals of time to evaluate progress? Are the measures reasonable? Are they reliable?

Relevant • There should be a clear and direct relationship between the objective and the manager's job. It should also be consistent with and related to organizational goals and higher-level objectives. How does it fit into the total set of job objectives? What other functions or activities are dependent upon its accomplishment? How does the objective support other organizational units or members? What is its contribution to the objectives of others?

Individual growth and development objectives for the coming period are also established during this step in the process. Since they are generally more personal in nature, they may be more difficult to deal with, depending upon the quality of relevant work relationships and the prevailing organizational climate. Meaningful personal development goals are based upon free and open communications, upon concern for human dignity and worth, upon trust and mutual respect, and upon an organizational climate which reflects an honest concern for the development of human potential. Personal development objectives should be set using the same guidelines and criteria used for performance objectives.

Step 5: Communicate and modify the objectives

Once the objectives have been formulated and expressed in written statements, they should be communicated to appropriate other members of the organization *and* modified as may be required. The manager can perhaps best accomplish this with a series of reviews or face-to-face discussions with his superior, his subordinates, and his peers.

Review with superior • The manager's supervisor reviews and discusses the pattern of objectives for clarity and for understanding. He looks for areas of omission or overlaps. He makes suggestions for modification. Although he has probably been actively involved throughout the process, this provides him with an opportunity to evaluate and "approve" the final product.

Review with subordinates • The manager should also review his objectives with each individual who reports to him. This provides the subordinates with an opportunity to express their own objectives and activities. In a sense, their own role awareness is expanded. They can also provide ideas and know the problems of implementation. They may also make some valuable suggestions to improve the final product.

Review with peers • The manager should also discuss his objectives with those on his own level. This provides an excellent opportunity to develop additional objectives to improve interfaces, to develop mutual support, and to facilitate horizontal coordination. It also provides an opportunity to make some important trade-offs.

It is important to stress at this point that this step, and every other in the above process, is a two-way street between the manager and those who have a relevant working relationship with him. The interaction between the man and his boss is especially critical. Many organizations find it both necessary and helpful to formalize the steps and to specify roles and relationships in the process. General Mills, for example, provides its managers with an excellent set of instructions for preparing job objectives.

In summary, then, individual job objectives should not be set in a vacuum. The process is an iterative one and requires meaningful interaction between the relevant parties. Adjustments and modifications are generally required along every step of the way. Although the process must be tailored to suit the needs and personalities of the managers involved, as well as the specific circumstances of the work environment, there are a number of useful points to remember.

First, individual job objectives are generally set once a year in most organizations. Although the time-frame for most objectives usually covers a one-year period, it may also include milestones and target dates. *Project* and *creative* objectives in particular are likely to include timelines and target dates which fall along different points throughout the year. As we shall see later, periodic progress reviews are generally conducted more frequently.

Second, MBO tends to be most effective when the emphasis is on *improvement* objectives. It may be useful, however, to establish maintenance objectives in some key areas to ensure that overall performance does not suffer as a result of the increased attention paid to those areas which are to be improved.

Third, there is no universally applicable balance or mix between routine, project, and creative job objectives. Depending upon the nature of the position, there may be more routine objectives and few, if any, project or creative objectives, or vice versa. Some organizations and managers believe that setting objectives in routine activities is hardly worth the effort (except perhaps to maintain a certain level of performance) and focus exclusively on special projects and creative activities.

Fourth, there is no magic number of job objectives that should be set for a given position. It is generally wise to limit the number of *improvement* objectives, especially in the first year. These may be increased as the individual gains more experience in managing by objectives. An "ideal" number and mix of managerial job objectives for the hypothetical plant manager described above might be, say, two each of routine, project, creative, and personal.

Fifth, it will be difficult to measure and quantify objectives in some areas and in some jobs. The important thing to remember is that objectives should be stated so that their attainment can be at least *verified*. It generally becomes easier to measure and quantify objectives as more experience is gained and as the organization improves its data base. At a minimum, "subjectives" may be used.

Sixth, our experience dictates that the impetus and responsibility for setting job objectives should rest with the individual manager since he's the one who knows his job best. His supervisor should play an active and vital role in helping him develop meaningful and significant objectives, but the quality of this interaction can be no better than the nature and quality of the relationship which normally exists between them.

ILLUSTRATIONS

As already indicated, there are many different methods and procedures for setting individual job objectives. There is an even greater number of different administrative forms and formats that can be used. They range from statements of objectives for the year typed on a plain piece of bond paper to sophisticated forms containing a complicated

FIGURE 4–2. A Simple Format.

Managerial Job Objectives			
<u>John Atkins</u> Prepared by the manager	<u>7/2</u> Date	<u>PLANT MANAGER</u> Manager's job title	
<u>F. W. Crawford</u> Reviewed by his supervisor	<u>7/2</u> Date	<u>PRESIDENT</u> Supervisor's job title	
Statement of Objectives Col. 1	P Col. 2	Date Col. 3	Outcomes or Results Col. 4
1. TO INCREASE DELIVERIES TO 98% OF ALL SCHEDULED DELIVERY DATES	A	6/31	
2. TO REDUCE WASTE AND SPOILAGE TO 3% OF ALL RAW MATERIALS USED.	A	6/31	
3. TO REDUCE LOST TIME DUE TO ACCIDENTS TO 100 MAN-DAYS/YEAR	B	2/1	
4. TO REDUCE OPERATING COST TO 10% BELOW BUDGET	A	1/15	
5. TO INSTALL A QUALITY CONTROL RADIOISOTOPE SYSTEM AT A COST OF LESS THAN $53,000	A	3/15	
6. TO IMPROVE PRODUCTION SCHEDULING AND PREVENTATIVE MAINTENANCE SO AS TO INCREASE MACHINE UTILIZATION TIME TO 95% OF CAPACITY	B	10/1	
7. TO COMPLETE THE UCLA EXECUTIVE PROGRAM THIS YEAR.	A	6/31	
8. TO TEACH A PRODUCTION MANAGEMENT COURSE IN UNIVERSITY EXTENSION	B	6/31	

network of categories, scales, blocks, and codes. Wikstrom (1968) and Humble (1970) provide numerous illustrations of the different forms used by some well-known companies in America and in Great Britain. A simple and flexible format is generally preferred when measurable results and standards of performance do not exist or are difficult to establish. This is especially true when a broad range of objectives, including new projects, special assignments, and subjectives, are to be included. Figure 4–2 is an example of one such relatively universal and flexible format. It provides for most of the data required to manage by objectives and is consistent with the process described above. Performance and personal development objectives are listed in column 1. It is essential with this format that they be stated precisely and in measurable or verifiable terms. A priority or relative weight of each objective is entered in column 2. The "A–B–C" priority system may be preferred when there are more than six or eight stated objectives. The expected completion date for each objective is then entered in column 3. These provide milestones and target dates against which to measure progress. The actual outcomes or results for the period are noted in column 4 during subsequent periodic performance reviews. Priorities may be changed, expected results modified, or target dates revised to meet changing requirements. The objectives established earlier for our hypothetical plant manager (see pp. 49 and 50) have been included to illustrate how such a format might be used.

When the achievement of objectives is more quantifiable and measurable and when meaningful standards of performance can be developed for the job, a more precise and less flexible format may be preferred. Figure 4–3 is one such example. It illustrates how a limited number of job functions and activities can provide the basis for meaningful objectives for a given managerial position. G. A. Robinson, the production manager, has identified the three most important result areas for his job. These are listed in column 1 as (1) product delivery, (2) product quality, and (3) operating efficiency. Other less important functions and activities were identified but, to simplify our discussion, will not be included.

He could have identified "quantity of units produced" as a major job activity or result area. However, the number of units produced may not mean as much to total organizational performance as getting the right numbers and kinds of units to the right customer at the right time and place. Meeting delivery schedules may contribute substantially more to sales potential and revenue. The important point of difference between the selected terms lies in their contribution to

FIGURE 4–3. Managerial Job Objectives.

G. A. Robinson — Date 12/1 — Prepared by Manager
Harold B. Williams — Date 12/15 — Reviewed by Supervisor

Position Title: PRODUCTION MANAGER
Position Title: V. P. MANUFACTURING

Progress Reviews
1. _____ Date
. . .
n _____ Date

MAJOR JOB FUNCTIONS, ACTIVITIES, OR KEY RESULT AREAS. Col. 1	% WT Col. 2	PERFORMANCE CRITERIA OR MEASURES OF RESULTS Col. 3	STD. OF PERF. Col. 4	RESULTS Target Col. 5a	RESULTS Actual Col. 5b	DATES Target Col. 6a	DATES Actual Col. 6b
1. PRODUCT DELIVERY (May be further broken down by products)	30%	a. Percent of monthly on-schedule delivery	95%	Increase to 97%		3/31	
		b. Number of customer delivery complaints as a % of monthly purchase orders	3%	Decrease to 2%		6/30	
2. PRODUCT QUALITY (May be further broken down by products)	25%	a. Percent of rejects per total monthly volume	5%	Decrease to 3%		5/31	
		b. Ratio of factory repair time to total production hours/month	8%	Decrease to 5%		7/31	
		c. Number of units service free during warranty period	74%	Increase to 85%		9/30	
3. OPERATING EFFICIENCY (May be further broken down by products)	20%	a. Cost per unit of output per month	$36.75/unit	Reduce to $35.50/unit		12/1	
		b. Equipment utilization time as a % of monthly available hours	85%	Increase to 90%		12/1	
N. OTHER KEY FUNCTIONS, ACTIVITIES, OR RESULT AREAS	25%						

overall organizational goals. Perhaps he knows from last year's performance that improvement in this area would be required to meet the company's sales and profit objectives.

In column 2 he has assigned his best estimate of the relative importance of each area as a percentage of its contribution to higher-level management objectives. The relative weighting provides a basis for resource allocation, budgeting, work planning, and responding to the demands made upon him by his supervisor and his subordinates. Note that he has assigned a relative weight of 75 percent to the three most important areas and only 25 percent to all of the other areas combined.

The performance indicators and criteria used to measure results are specified in column 3. The production manager, has, for example, selected "percent of monthly on-schedule delivery" and "number of customer delivery complaints as a percentage of monthly purchase orders" as indicators of product delivery. He may also decide to break it down by products to determine which ones offer the greatest potential for improvement. This may also be done in the other areas. He can then work with his subordinates to give emphasis to those products that can make the greatest contribution. Notice that he has developed more than one performance indicator for each of the three categories. It generally helps to identify as many meaningful and reliable result indicators as possible for each key area of performance.

The production manager has also established standards of performance for each result indicator. These appear in column 4. They are based on past levels of acceptable performance and provide the basis for his objectives and targets for the coming period.

His specific job objectives are contained in columns 5a and 6a under "Target Results" and "Target Dates." They are in keeping with the essential criteria of well-formulated objectives described earlier. Each target result is *relevant* because it is directly related to G. A. Robinson's job as a manager and makes a significant contribution to overall organizational goals and higher-level objectives. It is *measurable* because its achievement is based upon tangible and quantifiable results. And it is *challenging* because it represents a specific and significant improvement over past levels of performance. The target dates, on the other hand, assure that the objective is *attainable* by providing a reasonable time-frame for accomplishing the targeted results. The blank spaces (in columns 5b and 6b) are used to record the "actual" results and dates of achievement. These will be filled in by G. A. Robinson and his boss during the periodic progress reviews.

GUIDELINES

As most managers soon learn, it is a lot easier to talk about objectives than it is to structure them and to put them into writing. An objective, whether it be for the organization or for an individual, should be both well structured and well stated. It should actually communicate the author's intent to all relevant parties; the individual manager himself, who formulates the objectives for his job and his organization, the manager's supervisor, who must review and approve the objective, and the manager's subordinates and other organization members who will play a part in its achievement.

A well-stated objective is essentially a promise to do something, or to take some action, that will result in a measurable or verifiable accomplishment within a given period of time and at a specified cost. It specifies *action* and *results* within the specified *time* and *cost* constraints, as, for example, "to reduce product rejections (action) to five percent per thousand (results) by March 15 (time) within existing budget (cost)."

Notice that the format of a statement of objective deals with only the bare essentials. It specifies the "what," the "when," and the "how much" of the action and its anticipated results. It does not attempt to explain "why" the objective was selected or "how" it is to be attained. The "why" of it should have been dealt with by the participants in the goal-setting process. If it is necessary to put something in writing, a separate statement of rationale would be more appropriate. Similarly, the "how" of it is normally excluded from the statement of objective. The *means* of its accomplishment should be covered in the action plan (see Chapter 5). However, if there is only one acceptable means to achieve the objective, the "how" of it may be included in the statement. Our previous illustration might be changed to read as follows: "To reduce project rejections to five percent per thousand, through improved quality control procedures, by March 15 within existing budget."

A number of ground rules have been established to assist the manager in developing job objectives. Although a given objective may not satisfy all of the criteria, it should be consciously checked against each of the following guidelines to enhance its validity:

1) *It should specify the action to be taken.* The commitment to do something or to take some form of action is fundamental to any objective. Accomplishment must result from such action.

2) *It should focus on an identifiable target result.* It must be

clear to all concerned when the objective has or has not been achieved. For example, an objective "to increase sales of products *A, B,* and *C* ten percent each during the coming year within the existing sales budget" is poorly worded. Failure to achieve the objective for any one product implies failure to meet the total objective. If each of the three products is to have a sales target, then each should have a separate objective and perhaps a separate action plan. If not, and if one person can be held accountable for the sales of all three products, then the objective should read "to increase *total* sales of products *A, B,* and *C* by ten percent during the coming year within the existing sales budget."

3) *It should be time limited.* The accomplishment of the objective should be tied to a specified time-frame. That is, it must include either an implied or stated completion date. For some objectives the target date is assumed to be the end of the month, quarter, year, or forecast period. For others, however, a specific calendar date is established to help determine when the results are expected. Target dates also provide milestones against which to compare progress.

4) *It should specify cost.* While the cost factors associated with the accomplishment of some objectives either cannot be calculated or are not significant, each objective should be evaluated in terms of the resources which will be allocated to it. Measures such as dollars, man-hours, raw materials, machine-hours, and other opportunity costs help determine whether or not it is a worthwhile objective and provide a basis for evaluating how efficiently the action was accomplished. They also help in establishing priorities.

5) *It should be measurable, tangible, or verifiable.* To the extent possible, the objective should be expressed in measurable and tangible terms. This does not mean that all objectives can, or even should, be quantified. Numbers are tricky. They suggest a precision that might not exist. It takes skill to identify reasonably reliable indicators of performance. The wrong number is wrong even if it *looks* precise. What it does mean is that the objective should be stated in terms which are as specific and quantitative as possible. Providing the results are verifiable, the use of subjectives is suggested for those areas which are hard to quantify.

6) *It should be challenging.* The objective should represent a significant challenge to the man. It represents an improve-

ment over past performance. It destroys the status quo and points to growth and development. The focus is on change and improvement. As such, it should provide strong motivation to stretch beyond current levels of performance.

7) *It should be realistic and attainable.* Although a good objective is challenging, it should also be within reach of the manager. This means that it must either be within his competence or represent a reasonable learning and development experience for him. It should also be within his scope of authority. That is, he must be able to control or at least influence the results.

8) *It should be both relevant and important.* Since resources are limited, the attainment of the objective should provide a high payoff compared to others being considered.

9) *It should be consistent with organization plans, policies, and procedures.* The objective should not be in direct conflict with company policies or practices. If it does conflict with an existing policy, say the current practice of dealing with customer complaints, then one or the other will have to give. An assessment should be made to determine whether the practice is to be modified or the objective changed or abandoned for the time being.

10) *It should be put in writing and kept for future reference by the relevant parties.* Once formulated, the objective should be written down and referred to periodically by the manager, his supervisor, and any others who might have an interest or part in its attainment. This suggests that the statement must be written (A) in clear, concise, and unambiguous terms; (B) in a way which accurately specifies the "who," "what," and "how much"; and (C) in a language which will be understood by those who will play some part in the action planning, implementation, and review process.

SUMMARY

Setting objectives is perhaps the most critical phase of the MBO process. Valid and clearly stated objectives provide direction and focus for the remaining functions and activities of management. The manager who becomes meaningfully involved in a series of steps similar to those described above has a basis for more effective planning in his area of responsibility. The process of identifying and writing job objectives is deceptively simple. It can become just another "paper exercise" unless the individual manager follows some final words of advice:

1) Adapt your objectives directly to organizational goals and strategic plans. Do not *assume* that they support higher-level management objectives.

2) Quantify and target the results whenever possible. Do not formulate objectives whose attainment cannot be measured or at least verified.

3) Test your objectives for challenge and achievability. Do not build in cushions to hedge against accountability for results.

4) Adjust the objectives to the availability of resources and the realities of organizational life. Do not keep your head either in the clouds or in the sand.

5) Establish reliable performance reports and milestones that measure progress toward the objective. Do not rely on instinct or crude benchmarks to appraise performance.

6) Put your objectives in writing and express them in clear, concise, and unambiguous statements. Do not allow them to remain in loose or vague terms.

7) Limit the number of statements of objectives to the *most* relevant key result areas of your job. Do not obscure priorities by stating too many objectives.

8) Communicate your objectives to your subordinates so that they can formulate their own job objectives. Do not demand that they do your goal setting for you.

9) Review your statements with others to assure consistency and mutual support. Do not fall into the trap of setting your objectives in a vacuum.

10) Modify your statements to meet changing conditions and priorities.

11) Do not continue to pursue objectives which have become obsolete.

REFERENCES

Humble, J. W. *Management by Objectives in Action.* McGraw-Hill, 1970.

Odiorne, G. S. *Management by Objectives.* Pitman, 1965.

Wikstrom, W. S. *Managing by and with Objectives,* Studies in Personnel Policy, No. 212. National Industrial Conference Board, 1968.

Action Planning

5

THE NEED FOR ACTION PLANS

Clear, concise statements of objectives provide the basis for managing by and with objectives. They are expressions of expected results. While the statements reflect desired *ends,* however, they do not generally specify the *means* for their attainment. The "how" of the objective is the subject of action planning. Its focus is on specifying the methods or activities required to reach the desired end state. An action plan, then, is essentially a description of what is to be done, how, when, where, and by whom, and how much is required to reach a stated objective. It may be expressed as a brief summary statement of how the results are to be achieved, or, in the case of complex project or creative objectives, may be programmed into a series of major activities and events. Action plans are generally not developed for routine objectives.

Many of the potential problems of MBO can be avoided by systematic action planning. A well-conceived action plan facilitates the measurement of performance and progress. This is especially true when the objective is difficult to quantify. Since the activities specified in the action plan are presumed to lead to the desired outcome, we can assess progress during the implementation phase and can assume that the objective has been reached when all the activities or events have taken place.

Action plans provide many benefits. They offer an opportunity to test the feasibility of reaching objectives; they help identify potential

FIGURE 5–1.   MBO as a System: Step 5.

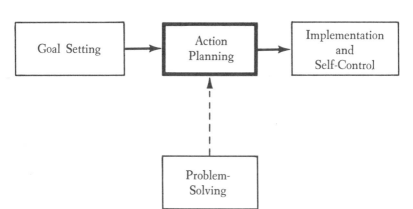

problem areas and unanticipated consequences; they facilitate the search for better and more efficient ways to achieve objectives; they provide a sound basis for estimating costs, schedules, and the nature and extent of required resources; they help to identify the nature of work relationships and support needed for other people in the organization; and they help to identify the contingencies upon which the successful attainment of an objective is based. In short, action planning facilitates the smooth transition from stated objectives to implementation of the activities leading to their achievement. As illustrated in Figure 5–1, action plans provide the connecting link between statements of objectives and the implementation phase of the MBO process.

DEVELOPING AN ACTION PLAN

Some objectives may be simple enough in approach that an elaborate program for their attainment is not necessary. If this is so, then a brief summary statement of how the objective is to be achieved may suffice. For example, action plan statements for objectives in the areas listed below might be expressed in the following manner:

A *sales increase*—"Develop greater market penetration in a given geographic area by increasing the number of calls to dealers there."

An improvement in product quality—"Reduce product rejections by improving quality control procedures."

A reduction in manufacturing costs—"Analyze overtime activities and costs and schedule more work during regular working hours."

Some project or creative objectives, however, can be accomplished more effectively and efficiently when they are subdivided or "programmed" into workable units of action. A well-conceived action plan lays out the principal steps or activities that must take place to achieve the objective (or set of objectives), identifies responsibilities for each step or activity, and specifies the schedule for its accomplishment. Skill in developing, testing, and implementing action plans is a major asset to any manager involved in managing by objectives. There are essentially seven basic steps that can be followed to facilitate the development of an action plan.

Step 1: Specify what is to be accomplished

The first requirement in planning an action is to know where you are going. That is, you must know what is to be accomplished and by what target date. The statement of objective provides an excellent first step. It provides the overall direction and the necessary end state toward which all planned activities are focused. When the president of a company decides to "increase return on investment to 15% after taxes by the end of next year," he provides the basis for derivative objectives in the key result areas and subareas. The vice-president of marketing, for example, might then decide "to increase sales volume by 10%" as one of his supporting objectives for next year. He has specified both a means and an end. An increase in sales volume is one of the things required to increase the return on investment, and is in itself an end result to be accomplished. It is a means to reaching the president's objective and an end to be achieved by the marketing department.

Step 2: Define the major activities required to support the objective

A chain of discrete activities or units of work forming the key action steps required to reach the desired objective should be clearly defined. This is essentially a continuation of the "means-end" decisions described above. Given the statement of objective, "to increase sales volume by 10% by the end of next year," the vice-president of marketing may decide on the following activities:

1) Release the new product which has been developed to augment the product line.

2) Evaluate the feasibility of a reduction in price to stimulate demand for the existing product line (products X and Y).

3) Upgrade the effectiveness of sales personnel in selected geographical areas.

4) Increase the rate of delivery for products X and Y.

It is helpful to define the purpose, the expected results, and the constraints and criteria for each major activity so as to provide a basis for programming specific action steps. The purpose of "upgrading the effectiveness of sales personnel," for example, may be to yield a higher dollar volume of purchase orders in the lower-performing regions. The expected result may be a five percent per month increase in the number of purchase orders over the next six months. The basic constraints and criteria might include holding the existing budget, increasing the average customer contact rate per day, conducting hard-hitting performance reviews and coaching sessions with each salesman, and upgrading the sales motivation media.

Step 3: Establish the critical relationships between the major activities

The emerging action plan becomes better defined when the connections and relationships between the major activities have been established. The sequencing of activities provides a basis for milestones and coordination and integration of each activity. Further analysis by the vice-president of marketing might result in the following sequence of action steps:

1) Increase the rate of delivery of products X and Y.

2) Reduce the price of our existing product line.

3) Upgrade the effectiveness of sales personnel in the Northeastern and Southern regions.

4) Release the new product.

The rationale for this sequence might follow this line of reasoning: "An increase in the rate of delivery of products X and Y will contribute to lower unit costs and set the stage for a price reduction without affecting profit margins. Lower prices will enable us to capture a larger share of the market, which will in turn be supported by the increased delivery rate. The increase in sales growth and sales commissions, coupled with effective coaching sessions, will set the climate for increasing the total effectiveness of our sales people. As they grow in their ability to sell, the stage will be set for the smooth entry of the new product into the market." In this manner derivative planning begins to take place. The sequence of major activities provides an important framework for establishing derivative objectives and action plans both downward and laterally across organizational lines.

Step 4: Clarify roles and relationships and assign primary responsibility for each activity

Work relationships between managers and departments within the organization must be clarified and primary responsibility for accomplishing each major activity should be assigned. This is especially true for higher-level management objectives and activities. An increase in the delivery rate of products, for example, may have consequences for the production and engineering functions. Changes in production volume, flow, pace, and the layout of facilities may be required. Who has primary responsibility for this phase of the program? What are the roles and relationships between the various functional managers? There are of course many ways to make these decisions. Later in this chapter we will describe a relatively simple and effective method for dealing with this problem. For the moment, however, we will simply assume that the following assignments were made by "top management" and have become part of our illustrative action plan:

Action steps	Primary responsibility
1) Increase rate of delivery	Production manager
2) Establish new price structure	Vice-president of marketing
3) Increase effectiveness of sales personnel	Sales manager
4) Release new product	Chief engineer

Step 5: Estimate time-lines for each major activity and its subactivities

The two main dimensions of time to be considered are the end target dates for completing each major step and subactivity and the amount of time required to complete the activity. The latter provides the basis for determining the most reasonable starting date. This requires a careful analysis of available resources to determine if each step and its subactivities can be realistically programmed and performed in a timely manner. Particular care must be exercised to ensure that sufficient start-up time has been provided for each activity.

There are numerous methods and techniques available to the manager for scheduling series of events. These range from the extremely complex PERT (Program Evaluation and Review Technique) to the simple practice of marking the dates and critical activity checkpoints on an ordinary calendar. To continue our illustration, we will assume that the time estimates for each of the major steps and their subactivities have been provided by the responsible parties and have been entered on a simple *milestone chart* by the vice-president of marketing. (See Figure 5-2.) He now has most of the ingredients that go into a well-conceived and well-programmed action plan.

Step 6: Identify additional resources required for each activity

It is important at this point to determine the type and amount of additional resources—facilities, materials, equipment, money, and manpower—that will be needed to implement the plan. How much of each will be required for each activity? What is their availability to support the schedule? A number of tradeoff decisions will have to be made based upon priorities, constraints, and the degree of flexibility inherent in the plan.

It is essential for the manager to look at costs *before* he is committed to a course of action. This gives him greater insight into the efforts he is planning. It enables him to determine whether it is worth pursuing what may initially have looked like a good objective. It also helps him develop and evaluate alternative ways to reach the objective.

This step reflects the "budgeting" aspects of action planning. As such, it provides a logical link between the MBO system and the organization's budgeting process. If the total management job is re-

FIGURE 5-2. A Simple Milestone Chart.

Major Activities, Tasks, and Events	Primary Responsibility	Month J F M A M J J A S O N D

1. Increase Delivery Rate.
  a. Subactivity 1
  b. Subactivity 2
  c. Subactivity 3
  d. Subactivity 4
	Production Manager	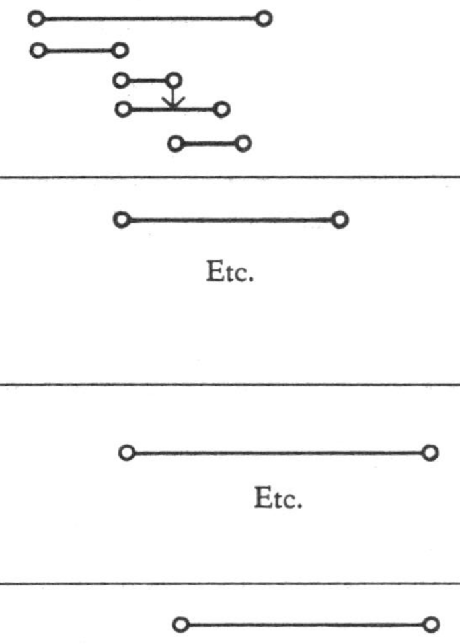

2. Establish New Price Structure.
  a. Subactivity 1
  b. Subactivity 2
  c. Subactivity 3
	Vice-President Marketing	Etc.

3. Increase Effectiveness of Sales Personnel.
  a. Subactivity 1
  b. Subactivity 2
	Sales Manager	Etc.

4. Release New Product.
  a. Subactivity 1
  b. Subactivity 2
  c. Subactivity 3
	Chief Engineer	Etc.

flected in a set of objectives, and if each objective has in turn been divided into programmed activities or events, it becomes a simple matter of logically estimating the cost of each activity to arrive at a total budget estimate. The exact nature of the connection and the extent of the relationship between action planning and the budgeting process will vary from organization to organization. The relationship may be vague and poorly defined, at least initially, or it may be an integral part, the backbone, of the process. It really depends upon how the organization chooses to allocate its resources.

Step 7: Verify deadlines and modify the action plan

The process of evolving and programming the required subactivities for each major activity may require several iterations. Deadlines and estimates will have to be verified or modified, and derivative plans may have to be formulated. The integrity of the action plan is maintained only when the plan is specific and realistic, when responsibility has been accepted, when accountability has been established, when there is commitment to the objectives, and when discretionary authority has been sufficiently delegated to get the job done.

In summary, then, action planning provides the connecting link between the "ends" and the "means" of managing by objectives. The action plan itself may be reflected in a brief summary statement or in a more comprehensive plan of major activities and events programmed to achieve the objective. The seven-step process described above provides the manager with a systematic way to respond to the need for action planning as an integral part of his job.

MANAGING RESPONSIBILITY

One of the critical steps in action planning is assigning responsibility for the major tasks or activities required to reach a set of objectives. A second critical step is clarifying interfaces and work relationships. This is particularly true when the objectives require functions and activities that cut across organizational lines and clouded and ambiguous questions are consequently raised. Who should be involved in which activity? What is the nature of the interface between various organization members? Who should be held responsible for which part of the plan? What is the nature of that responsibility? The management of responsibility in MBO should be approached in a logical, systematic manner, in a way which will enable management to see and resolve potential role conflicts before they actually occur.

The conventional tools of management have not been very effective in dealing with the questions of responsibility and accountability in organizations. Job descriptions, for example, are generally broad statements of what an individual is expected to do. They do not adequately describe the nature of the interfaces between one managerial position and another. Nor can they keep up with the requirements of a dynamic and rapidly changing environment. The same limitations apply to organization charts. Although they are excellent tools for delineating the formal hierarchical structure, or the "pecking order" of who reports to whom, they do not tell the full story. They do not show the complexity of the interfaces and work relationships between managerial positions. And, like job descriptions, their usefulness is generally limited to relatively stable organizational environments.

Linear Responsibility Charts may provide a better basis for dealing with the question of roles and responsibilities in organizations (for a description, see "Linear responsibility charting," *Factory*, 1963). This is essentially a technique designed to describe and relate management positions to functions and responsibilities. When coupled with a way of describing the nature of the work relationships, it is far superior to either an organization chart or a job description. A number of slightly different approaches and formats have emerged over the past decade or so. The *Managerial Responsibility Guide* (MRG) is perhaps among the best-known responsibility charting techniques (for a description, see Melcher, 1967).

With some modifications, responsibility charting provides an effective tool for dealing with the question of accountability and responsibility in MBO. The major activities and tasks required to achieve an objective or a set of objectives are listed on the left side of a matrix similar to the one illustrated in Figure 5–3. The names of individuals (or management positions) who are in some way concerned with a given activity or task are entered across the top of the matrix. The coded relationship that each manager or position has with regard to an activity or task is then determined and entered at the appropriate intercept. The MRG approach, for example, uses the following codes to describe the nature of the relationships (Melcher, 1967, p. 35):

A = *General responsibility*: The individual guides and directs the execution of a function through the person delegated oper-

FIGURE 5–3. An Illustration of a Responsibility Matrix.

Objective:

"To increase sales volume by 10% by the end of next year."

Management Position

Responsibility codes

A = General responsibility

B = Operating responsibility

C = Specific responsibility

D = Must be consulted

E = May be consulted

F = Must be notified

G = Must approve

Major Activities/Tasks	President	V.P. Marketing	Sales Manager	V.P. Manufacturing	Production Manager	Quality Control Engineering	V.P. Finance R and D	Personnel Manager	Regional Sales Manager
1. Increase the rate of delivery of products X and Y.	A B	C	D	D	F	F			F
2. Revise the price structure of existing products.	A	B C	D			F	F		F
3. Upgrade the effectiveness of sales personnel in the northeast and southern regions.	A	B					D	C	
4. Release the new product.	G A F		D	D	C	B			

ating responsibility and has approval authority over the function.

B = *Operating responsibility:* The individual is directly responsible, at the operating level, for execution of the function.

C = *Specific responsibility:* The individual is delegated responsibility for execution of a specific or limited portion of the function.

D = *Must be consulted:* The individual, if decision affects his area, must be called in prior to any decision being made, or approval granted, to confer, render advice, or relate information, but does not make the decision or grant approval.

E = *May be consulted:* The individual may be called in to confer, relate information, render advice, or make recommendations.

F = *Must be notified:* The individual must be notified of action that has been taken.

G = *Must approve:* The individual (other than persons holding general and operating responsibility) must grant approval.

This figure illustrates how a responsibility matrix might be used as part of an action plan to meet one of the objectives of our marketing vice-president. The major activities required to meet his sales volume objective have been entered on the left of the matrix. Those individuals or management positions that might have a working relationship with any given activity are listed across the top. A slightly modified code has been used to describe the nature of the relationships vis-à-vis the activities. Needless to say, the details of the process and the way in which potential conflicts are raised and handled vary with the circumstances. It may be desirable in some instances for the head of the management team to assign the responsibility codes without the involvement of the other members. In most situations, however, it is best to involve the relevant members of the team in all phases of the process. This provides an excellent vehicle for clarifying roles and responsibilities around group and individual objectives.

CLARIFYING AUTHORITY

The general problem of determining roles and relationships in MBO may involve more than just the assignment of responsibility for specified activities and tasks. It may also require a clarification of the distribution of authority within the organization. More specifically, the individual manager may find it helpful to examine the action plan in the light of the degree of authority which has been delegated to him. What is the nature of his authority to carry out the various elements of the action plan? What are some of the limitations upon the activities and tasks required to meet the objectives? The answers to questions such as these can be found in the systematic analysis of the degree of authority which has been delegated to him in connection with each of the various activities and subactivities specified in the action plan.

A variation of the linear responsibility charting techniques may be used to facilitate the analysis. As in the case of the responsibility chart, the activities and subactivities required to reach the objectives are listed on the left side of a matrix similar to the one illustrated in Figure 5–4. The nature and extent of authority the individual manager has in connection with each action is entered across the top of the matrix. The varying degrees of managerial authority could be described in any number of ways, including the following:

A = He has complete authority to make decisions and to take whatever actions are required to carry out the activity or to complete the task.

B = He has complete authority to decide or to act, but must inform someone of his decisions and actions.

C = He has the authority to make decisions or to take actions, but must first coordinate or consult with someone.

D = He has the authority to take action only with the prior approval of some other person.

E = He must be consulted prior to the action, but the decision comes to him from another manager or position.

F = He must be notified of the decision or action taken to carry out the activity.

To facilitate the analysis, the manager places an X in the inter-cept which best describes his degree of authority to make decisions or to take action in each specified area. This gives him a good sense of the overall nature of his authority in implementing the action plan. He also enters the names or the positions of those who must be informed or consulted, or from whom he must seek approval or direction. More than one name or position can be entered for a given activity to provide him

FIGURE 5–4. An Authority Analysis Matrix.

Objective:

"To increase sales volume by 10% by the end of next year."

Major Activities/Tasks	Nature and amount of my authority						Comments
	A. I have complete authority to decide and to act.	B. I have complete authority but must notify ___.	C. I have complete authority but must first consult with ___.	D. I need the prior approval of ___.	E. I must consult with me first.	F. I must notify me of action taken.	
1. Increase the rate of delivery of products X and Y		Production manager	V.P. mfg. ✗				Get inputs from and notify all regional sales managers.
2. Revise the price structure of existing products		V.P. finance	President ✗				Notify the sales manager of the coming changes.
3. Upgrade the effectiveness of sales personnel in the north-eastern and southern regions	✗	Personnel manager					Delegate this activity to the re-gional sales managers.
4. Release the new product			President	R & D ✗			Consult with production man-ager for product schedules and delivery dates.

with more insight into the nature of his authority. A section is provided on the right-hand side of the matrix for additional comments or entries. The authority matrix adds another dimension to the management of responsibility in MBO. It provides the individual manager with an opportunity to examine his action plan in the light of his overall authority to carry out the plan. As such, it provides another vehicle for identifying potential conflicts and for clarifying roles and relationships in carrying out the tasks and activities required to meet the objectives.

Figure 5–4 also illustrates how an authority matrix might be filled out by our marketing vice-president. The reader may have already noted the similarity between the two matrices (see Figure 5–3). They are in reality different sides of the same coin. The focus of the responsibility matrix is on the management *team* and the nature of each member's accountability for a given activity or task. The focus of the authority matrix, on the other hand, is on the *individual* manager and the relationship between his delegated authority and its impact on his ability to make decisions or to take action in each of the activities required to implement his action plans.

SUMMARY

Managing responsibility and clarifying authority relationships are important by-products of action planning and managing by objectives. Activities of this sort are especially useful for new management teams, or when one or more new members have joined the team, or where lines of authority and responsibility are fuzzy or unclear, or in a turbulent and rapidly changing environment. It should be noted that these conditions are likely to exist in *any* organization and not just those with an MBO system. The approaches described here represent structured and relatively simple ways of improving task relationships. "Team building" activities, both structured and unstructured, are more and more becoming a way of life in modern organizations (more detailed accounts of team building and other organizational development activities may be found in, e.g., Margulies and Raia, 1972).

REFERENCES

"Linear responsibility charting." *Factory* (March 1963): 88–91.
Margulies, N., and A. P. Raia. *Organizational Development: Values, Process, and Technology.* McGraw-Hill, 1972.
Melcher, R. D. "Roles and relationships: Clarifying the manager's job." *Personnel* 44 (May-June 1967): 33–41.

Implementation
and Self~Control

MANAGERIAL CONTROL
THROUGH SELF-CONTROL

The exercise of *control* is the crucial connecting link between putting plans into action and the attainment of desired results (see Figure 6–1). Managerial control involves measuring progress and performance and, when necessary, taking corrective action to assure that the objectives are achieved. This generally requires sound data and appropriate feedback mechanisms (i.e., an effective information system).

Traditionally, the focus of managerial control has been on controlling the activities of *other* people. Human response to external control may range from complete compliance to utter rebellion. Management's reactions, in turn, are in the form of administrative trappings and extrinsic rewards and punishments. Although these may result in some degree of compliance on the part of organization members, they can also yield widespread antagonism toward the controls (and to those who impose them), a high degree of resistance, higher administrative costs, and the necessity for closer supervision. The manager who exercises control over other people can be no more effective than a back-seat driver.

There are a number of propositions about management and

82

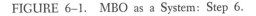

FIGURE 6–1.   MBO as a System: Step 6.

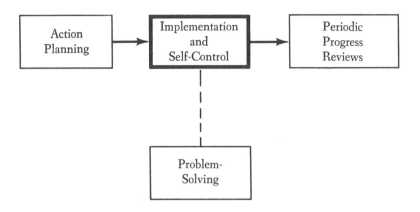

assumptions about human nature which underlie the carrot-and-stick approach to managerial control. They have been labeled *Theory X* by McGregor (1960), and may be summarized as follows:

> 1) *Management* is responsible for organizing the elements of productive enterprise—money, materials, equipment, and people—in the interest of economic ends.
>
> 2) *Management* is a process of directing the efforts of other people, motivating them, controlling their actions, and modifying their behavior to fit the needs of the organization.
>
> 3) Without this active intervention by *management*, people would be passive—even resistant—to organizational needs. They must therefore be persuaded, rewarded, punished, and controlled. Their activities must be directed.
>
> 4) The average *human being* is by nature indolent—he works as little as possible.
>
> 5) He lacks ambition, dislikes responsibility, and prefers to be led.
>
> 6) He is inherently self-centered and is consequently indifferent to organizational needs.
>
> 7) He is by nature resistant to innovation and change.
>
> 8) He is gullible, not very bright, the ready dupe of the charlatan and the demagogue.

As indicated earlier, however, management by objectives rests heavily upon the concept of self-control, not control over people, but rather control over operations. If the manager has participated in setting goals and objectives for his area of responsibility, he knows *what* he is supposed to do; he knows *how* to do it if he has been involved in action planning. Provided he gets the information and feedback he needs, he can measure his own progress and take whatever corrective action may be required to attain his objectives. He does not have to rely on his boss to let him know how he is doing.

The integration of individual needs and organizational goals in MBO, then, requires a different theory about management and human nature. Theory X assumptions about the nature of modern man, with his increasing level of education and standard of living, are generally inaccurate. Managerial controls which develop from these assumptions will often fail to motivate individuals to work for organizational goals. McGregor felt that management practices based on a more accurate understanding of modern management and the nature of man were needed. His alternate theory of human behavior, labeled *Theory Y*, assumes that people are not inherently lazy and irresponsible. In fact, properly motivated, man can be creative and is both self-directed and self-controlled. He often finds that he can satisfy his own needs best by directing his own efforts toward accomplishing organizational goals. *Theory Y* propositions and assumptions might be summarized as follows:

1) *Management* is responsible for organizing the elements of productive enterprise—money, materials, equipment, and people—in the interest of economic ends.

2) *People* are *not* by nature passive or resistant to organizational needs. They have become so as a result of their experience in organizations.

3) The motivation, the potential for development, the capacity for assuming responsibility, the readiness to direct behavior toward organizational goals arc all present in people. *Management* does not put them there. It is a responsibility of management to make it possible for people to recognize and develop these human characteristics for themselves.

4) The essential task of *management* is to arrange organizational conditions and methods of operation so that people can achieve their own goals *best* by directing *their own* efforts toward organizational objectives.

5) The expenditure of physical and mental effort in work is as natural as play or rest. The *average human being* does not

inherently dislike work. Depending upon controllable conditions, work may be a source of satisfaction (and will be voluntarily performed) or a source of punishment (and will be avoided if possible).

6) External control and the threat of punishment are not the only means of bringing about effort toward organizational objectives. *People* will exercise self-direction and self-control in the service of objectives to which they are committed.

7) Commitment to objectives is a function of the rewards associated with their achievement. The most significant of such rewards—the satisfaction of ego and self-actualization needs—can be direct products of effort directed toward organizational objectives.

8) The *average human being* learns, under proper conditions, not only to accept but to seek responsibility. Avoidance of responsibility, lack of ambition, and emphasis on security are generally consequences of experience, not inherent human characteristics.

9) The capacity to exercise a relatively high degree of imagination, ingenuity, and creativity in the solution of organizational problems is *widely,* not narrowly, distributed in the population.

10) Under the conditions of modern industrial life, the intellectual potentialities of the *average human being* are only partially utilized.

Management by objectives and self-control, then, is based upon a set of humanistic assumptions about the nature of man in organizations. It also involves a number of other essential ingredients, including highly motivated managers, a motivating work environment, and the active involvement and participation in the MBO process by managers at all levels.

HUMAN NEEDS AND MOTIVES

Behavior in organizations is generally a function of *both* the person and his environment. Each individual has a unique and complex pattern of needs, wants, desires, drives, and motives. Some are conscious or active, others are unconscious or dormant. They stem from inside the individual and cause him to behave in ways that will satisfy them. They are subject to change over time. They are also subject to change with the situation. The external environment may stimulate or arouse some needs and stifle or limit others. Together, an individual's pattern of needs and the environment he works in produce the behavior we see.

Need theory

Abraham Maslow (1954) provides a conceptual framework which many practicing managers have found to be most useful. According to Maslow, man is a perpetually wanting creature. As soon as one need is satisfied, another rushes in to take its place. Furthermore, they can be arranged in a hierarchy of "prepotency" or importance to the individual. This means that the more important needs dominate his conscious life and serve to stimulate his behavior. The less important needs tend to be minimized and may even be forgotten or denied. When a given need is fairly well satisfied, however, the next prepotent (or "higher-level") need emerges to dominate his behavior. Maslow's "hierarchy of needs" is graphically illustrated in Figure 6–2 and may be summarized as follows:

Physiological needs • Physical and physiological needs are the most basic needs of man. At the lowest level in the hierarchy, but of highest importance when they are not satisfied, are the classic human needs to sustain life itself. Until the need for food and other essentials— clothing, rest, exercise, sex, shelter, etc.—is satisfied, behavior is almost always focused at this level. Man does not live by bread alone unless there is no bread. Higher-level needs are inoperative when the stomach is empty.

Security needs • Once the physiological needs are reasonably well satisfied, needs at the next higher level begin to dominate his behavior, to motivate him. These are the security or safety needs. They are essentially the needs for self-preservation and protection against danger and deprivation. There is also concern for the future. When a man is in a dependent relationship and fears deprivation or feels threatened, his greatest needs are for protection against the threat, for guarantees, for security. Other things become less important.

Social needs • Once provision has been made to gratify the lower-level needs, social or love needs become important motivators of man's behavior. His needs for acceptance, for belonging, for association, and for friendship and love will cause him to search for and cultivate

FIGURE 6–2. The Hierarchy of Needs.

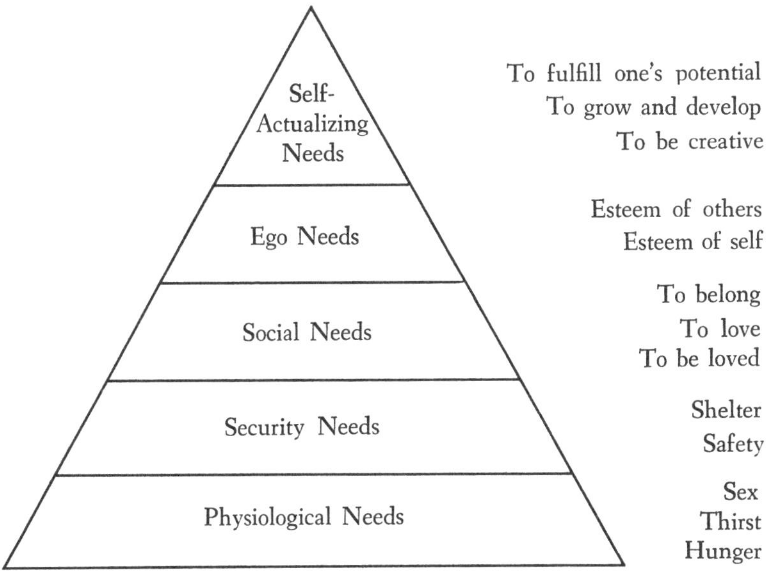

satisfying relationships with other people—a sweetheart, a wife and children, friends, and a variety of groups at work and in the community. Most of us find gratification in intimate associations with other people and feel genuinely deprived when these needs are not satisfied.

Ego needs • Above the social needs—in the sense that they do not become motivators until the lower-level needs are reasonably satisfied—are the egoistic or esteem needs. They are of two types: those that relate to one's self-esteem, e.g., the needs for independence, accomplishment, and a sense of self-worth and competence; and those that relate to one's reputation, e.g., the needs for the esteem of others, recognition, appreciation, and status. Unlike the lower-level needs, ego needs are never really satisfied. Man continuously seeks to satisfy these needs once they have become important to him.

Self-actualizing needs • The capstone of man's hierarchy of needs is the need for self-actualization or self-fulfillment. These highest-level needs generally consist of the need to realize one's full potential, to become everything that one is capable of becoming; a desire to grow and to develop through challenging and continuing self-development:

and the need to be creative in the broadest possible sense. As Maslow expressed it, "What a man *can* be, he *must* be." Self-actualization, however, is a process rather than an end state or a condition. The self-actualizing person may be described as one who is in the process of "becoming," of growing and developing toward his full potential as a human being. He is making full use of all his talents and abilities. He has a good sense of his strengths and weaknesses, and relies on his own inner resources for self-development. He utilizes independent thought and action when it is consistent with his competences and when it matters to him personally. He actively searches for new and challenging experiences in his never-ending quest for self-realization and fulfillment.

FIGURE 6–3.   Changing Patterns of Human Needs.
               Source: D. Krech and R. S. Crutchfield, 1958, p. 627.
               Reprinted by permission of the authors.

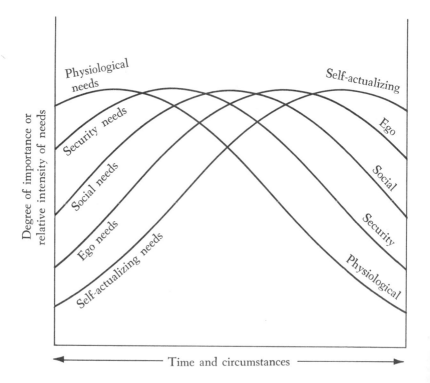

Maslow's framework provides some useful insights into human motivation and organizational behavior. As indicated earlier, however, each person has a *unique* and *complex* pattern of needs which is subject to change with time and with circumstances. Some of the key relationships are illustrated in Figure 6-3 and lead to the following observations:

1) There is a general tendency for man's pattern of needs to move from left to right (in the figure) in much the manner described above. As a person grows and matures psychologically, the lower-level needs become less important as the higher-level needs begin to dominate his behavior.

2) A given level of needs is never completely gratified, nor is it completely dormant or inoperative. The dominating set of needs does not have to be satiated before the next set emerges. The needs of most people are only partially satisfied or unsatisfied. To illustrate, a person could be described as 90 percent gratified in his physiological needs, 75 percent satisfied in his security needs, 55 percent in his social needs, 50 percent in his ego needs, and 35 percent in his needs to be self-actualizing. The relative degree of satisfaction varies with each individual depending upon time and circumstances.

3) Needs are almost never permanently satisfied. Dominating higher-level needs, for example, may quickly become less important to a person when he is faced with losing his job or is threatened with deprivation of some lower-level needs. Circumstances play an important part in determining an individual's pattern of needs at any given point in time.

Other psychologists, notably David C. McClelland (1961), have focused on some of the more "hidden" motives underlying human behavior in organizations. Among those that appear to be most important for practicing managers are the need to achieve (n–Ach), the need for affiliation (n–Aff), and the need for power (n–Pow). The relative intensity of each of these motives, which varies from individual to individual, has been scientifically identified and measured by McClelland and others.

The achievement motive • The need to achieve is the desire to be successful and to avoid failure. The high-need achiever is a man who spends most of his time thinking of ways to do a better job, accomplishing something important or unusual, and advancing his career. He is oriented toward solving the problem and getting the job done. And he has a high concern for doing it well. He thinks not only about achieving his goals, but about how he can attain them, about what obstacles he might encounter, and about how he will feel if he succeeds or fails.

A person with a strong achievement motive tends to search for and do well in jobs of an entrepreneurial nature. He makes a good manager and is generally the backbone of most organizations. Years of careful empirical research allow us to characterize his behavior, particularly as it relates to managing by objectives, along the following lines:

1) He tends to set moderately difficult, but realistic and attainable, goals for himself. He gets little satisfaction from doing a routine task or reaching an easy goal. On the other hand, an extremely difficult problem is likely to frustrate rather than satisfy his need to achieve success and to avoid failure. He likes to be challenged and tends to work harder under these conditions.

2) Given his need for accomplishment and his tendency to set challenging goals, he prefers to take calculated risks. There must be some real chance of not succeeding, but it must not be so great that he can't overcome it by his own efforts. He tries to find concrete ways to reduce risk and to avoid gambling where he cannot control the outcome.

3) He prefers to assume personal responsibility for achieving the goal or solving the problem. He is generally self-confident. When it comes to difficult or unknown tasks, he would rather rely on his own ability and believes he is more able than most others to do the job well.

4) He also wants concrete feedback on how well he is doing. Otherwise, how can he get any satisfaction out of what he has done? He has a compelling interest to know if he has done well or poorly, if he was right or wrong. And he likes to get the feedback as often and as soon as possible.

The affiliation motive • Like achievement motivation, the need for affiliation is a two-sided coin. It is the desire to experience the pleasure of being loved, of feeling needed and wanted. It is also the need to avoid the pain of being rejected. There is generally a high concern for intimacy and understanding in interpersonal relationships. The man who spends a good deal of time thinking about the warm and friendly relationships he has, or would like to have, has a high need for affiliation. He is concerned about establishing and maintaining positive emotional relationships with other people. When social relationships are disrupted, he is concerned about restoring or replacing them. He is likely to console or help someone in trouble. And he enjoys friendly social activities such as parties, reunions, and "bull sessions."

People with a strong affiliation motive are likely to pay attention to the feelings and needs of others. They tend to seek out jobs which offer an opportunity for friendly social interaction. They generally gravitate toward the institutionalized "helping" roles and professions such as nursing, counseling, and teaching. Those who find themselves in managerial positions, however, tend to prefer jobs where maintaining good relationships is more important than task-oriented decision-making.

Although a strong need for affiliation may not seem to be important for effective managerial performance, and in fact might well be detrimental if it is the sole source of motivation, current research suggests that some minimal concern for the feelings of others and for friendly relationships is necessary for effective management. Such a basic affiliative concern is essential for *interpersonal competence* in management. The manager who understands the needs of other members of the organization and builds good working relationships with them can expect more collaboration on their part. His behavior speaks for itself. It says that other people, as individuals *and* as sources of ideas, are involved in the management process.

The power motive • The need for power is generally concerned with exercising influence and control over other people. At one level it may be characterized by the *dominance* of one individual and the *submission* of others; he derives satisfaction from manipulating and controlling the activities of others to suit his own purpose. The relationship is essentially exploitative. At another level, however, the power motive may be characterized by a concern for group goals, for helping the group to identify and formulate them, for taking the initiative in providing group members with the means for their attainment, and for providing the group with the sense of strength and competence its members need to work together in an effective manner.

People with a strong need for power will usually attempt to influence others directly by giving their opinions, by making suggestions, and by arguing persuasively. They seek positions of leadership in group activities. They usually express themselves well, and tend to be talkative, sometimes even argumentative. They are often seen by others as being forceful and outspoken. They can also be hardheaded and demanding. As one might expect, they prefer jobs and positions which provide an opportunity to exercise power. They enjoy teaching, public speaking, and other activities that require persuasion. Because of their need to control the means of influence over other people, many gravitate toward public office and top management positions.

Current research indicates that the way in which the individual uses power depends less upon the strength of the motive and more upon his other needs and values. If he has a high need for power, but a low need for affiliation and strong authoritarian values, his behavior might tend to be dominating, manipulative, and exploitative. If, on the other hand, his high need for power is accompanied by a high need for affiliation and strong democratic values, his behavior might be oriented toward initiating ideas and inspiring others to be more active in group activities.

Since different motivations lead to different patterns of behavior, it is important that management learns to recognize and deal with basic human needs and motives as an integral part of the goal-setting and self-control process. Every individual is both unique and complex. Management must learn to tailor each job in a way which facilitates integrating the goals of the organization with the needs and motives of the individual. MBO provides an excellent vehicle for this integration, but its successful implementation depends upon management's ability to selectively arouse and satisfy the kind of motivation that leads to appropriate job behavior.

Dual-factor theory

Another approach to human behavior, well-known among practitioners, is that developed by Frederick Herzberg (1966) and his associates (1959). The "dual-factor" approach provides management with some additional insights into the relationship between the individual and his work environment. Herzberg's motivation-hygiene theory is the result of an interesting series of studies about job attitudes in a wide variety of organizations. Extensive interviews were conducted with a large number of people in different occupations to determine what job events had led to extreme satisfaction or dissatisfaction on their part.

Based upon these and other studies, Herzberg concludes that man has essentially two different sets of needs, one of which stems from his animal nature, which includes an inherent drive to avoid pain from the environment plus all the learned drives to satisfy the basic biological needs. The other set of needs stems from his human drive to achieve and to experience psychological growth. These two different categories of needs are essentially independent of each other and affect behavior in different ways. When respondents felt dissatisfied about their jobs, they seemed to be concerned about the environment in which they were working. On the other hand, when they felt good about their jobs, they identified things which had to do with the nature of the work itself. Herzberg calls the first category of needs "hygiene factors" because they describe the work environment and serve to prevent job dissatisfaction. He calls the second category "motivator factors" because they seem to lead to job satisfaction and to be effective in motivating people to superior performance.

Hygiene factors • Company policies and administration, technical supervision, interpersonal relationships, working conditions, money, status, security, and the like may be thought of as hygiene factors. They are *extrinsic,* or external, to the job and are related to the conditions under which the work is done. In this sense they are "preventive" and environmental. They are necessary but not sufficient for motivation. They do not make a person healthy; like water purification, they just keep him from becoming sick.

Motivator factors • Achievement, recognition for achievement, the nature of the work itself, responsibility, and opportunity for growth and advancement contribute most to job satisfaction and superior performance. They are *intrinsic* or inherent in the job itself. When satisfied, hygiene factors tend to eliminate or prevent dissatisfaction but do little to motivate an individual. Motivators, on the other hand, provide an opportunity for individual growth and improved performance.

Herzberg challenges management to create a work environment which provides an opportunity to satisfy the motivators. Job enlargement is not the answer. What management really needs to do, he suggests, is to *enrich* the job. This involves a deliberate upgrading of the responsibility, scope, and challenge of the work. The philosophy and process of management by objectives provide just such a vehicle.

Although the dual-factor theory of motivation is derived from empirical evidence, it is not without its critics. Subsequent studies have shown that certain dimensions of the job appear to be more important for both satisfaction and dissatisfaction (see, for example, House and Wigdor, 1967). Achievement, recognition, and responsibility, for example, were found to be important for both, while dimensions such as salary, security, and working conditions appear to be less important. Other studies have indicated that some workers are motivated by hygiene factors and others by motivators.

There are some distinct similarities and differences between the Maslow and Herzberg theories of motivation. Herzberg's hygiene factors tend to relate to Maslow's lower-level needs (social, security, and physiological), while his motivators tend to relate to the higher-level needs (ego and self-actualizing). Where Maslow assumes that any unsatisfied need can be a motivator, however, Herzberg argues that only higher-level needs serve as motivators, and that unsatisfied needs can exist simultaneously in both the hygiene and motivator areas. One might also note that neither theory provides a link between the satisfaction of individual needs and the attainment of organizational goals and objectives. It is entirely possible in both cases to satisfy needs which are not necessarily directed at achieving organizational objectives. Perhaps most important, however, neither approach adequately deals with the uniqueness of the individual.

Path-goal theory

The path-goal approach to human motivation provides an explicit link between need satisfaction, motivation, and organizational goals. The idea was suggested as early as 1955 by Brayfield and Crockett (1955), who said:

> It makes sense to us to assume that individuals are motivated to achieve certain environmental goals and that the achievement of these goals results in satisfaction. Productivity is seldom a goal in itself but is more commonly a means to goal attainment. Therefore, . . . we might expect high satisfaction and high productivity to occur together when productivity is perceived as a path to certain important goals and when these goals are achieved (p. 416).

Some early empirical support for this notion was provided by Georgopoulas et al. (1957) in their "path-goal hypothesis." These authors suggest that the motivation of an individual to produce at a given level depends upon how his particular needs are reflected in the goals toward which he is moving and upon his perception of how useful his behavior is as a path toward attaining these goals. However, they qualify this by noting that no other economical paths must be available, that the need must be sufficiently high, and that restraining practices must not get in the way.

More recently, Vroom (1964) has broadened this notion into a "preference-expectancy" theory of motivation. The concept is graphically illustrated in Figure 6–4. The model shows that the individual is faced with a set of alternative "first-level outcomes." His preference among these first-level outcomes is determined by his perception of their relationship to possible "second-level outcomes," by the extent to which first-level outcomes are seen as leading to second-level outcomes. *Valence* refers to the strength of an individual's desire for a particular outcome. The valence of a first-level outcome is directly related to the valences of all second-level outcomes and the extent to which the individual perceives that it will lead to their attainment.

Assume, for example, that an individual believes that high performance (first-level outcome) will lead to a desired promotion (second-level outcome). High performance acquires a positive valence because of its expected relationship to the preferred second-level outcome of promotion. If we further assume that there are no negative second-level outcomes associated with high performance (such as falling into disfavor with coworkers) and that there are no other first-level outcomes that will lead to promotion, we can expect the individual to be motivated to high performance.

Expectancy concerns the likelihood that a particular effort will be followed by a given first-level outcome and can be expressed as a subjective probability. Expectancy relates efforts or behavior to first-level outcomes. Simply stated, then, the central concept underlying this approach is that an individual's motivation (*force*) to engage in a specific behavior (*action*) is a function of two things, the personal satisfaction (*valence*) that he believes he will derive from a specific outcome and his expectation (*expectancy*) that the behavior will lead to that outcome. This approach to motivation is one which emphasizes individual differences and provides an opportunity to examine the explicit relationships between the attainment of organizational goals and motivation.

Management by objectives is consistent with the path-goal theory of motivation. The establishment of clearly defined work objectives, the periodic progress reviews, the tie between performance appraisals and manager training and compensation, as well as the participative nature of the process, all help clarify path-goal relationships, a result which, according to House (1971), has a positive motivational effect in that it reduces role ambiguity and makes it possible to use externally

FIGURE 6–4.   Preference-Expectancy Model. A Possible Model of Human Motivation Based on Vroom, 1964 (Dunnette, 1967).

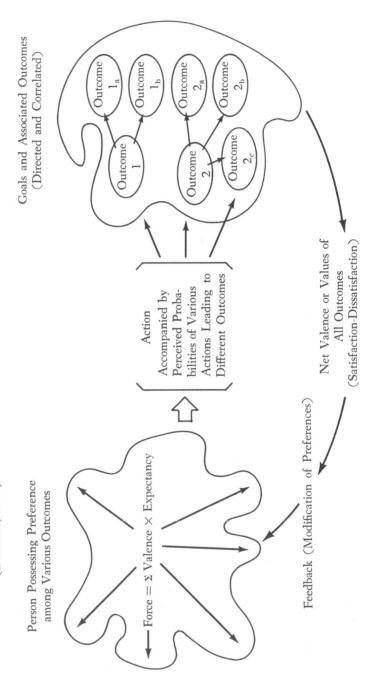

imposed controls. Role ambiguity has a negative valence (i.e., is a de-motivator) and tends to obscure the link between first and second-level outcomes. External controls can be motivational if they link personal satisfaction to desirable behavior, but, as House notes, externally imposed controls lead to improved performance only to the extent that rewards have a positive valence, that punishments have a negative valence, that rewards and punishments are contingent on performance, and that this contingency is clearly perceived by the individual. Whether or not the behavior is actually satisfying to the individual depends upon his latent motives and needs. Among other things, House suggests that the leadership function is essentially a matter of increasing the personal satisfactions to subordinates for attaining work goals and making the road to these pay-offs easier to travel—by clarifying the path, reducing the roadblocks, and increasing the opportunities for personal satisfaction along the way. MBO provides an opportunity for this to take place.

MANAGING MOTIVATION

As indicated earlier, there is an important distinction between a "latent" motive and "aroused" motivation. The former represents a relatively stable characteristic *within* an individual, while the latter results from the *situation* in which he finds himself. The distinction is an important one. It means that individual motivation in organizations can actually be influenced by the work environment. Litwin and Stringer (1968), for example, provide some interesting research on the impact of organizational climate on motivation. One of their studies involved creating organizations with different climate characteristics and testing their impact on the achievement, affiliation, and power motives of people in a laboratory setting. Each of the organizations was designed to arouse one of the three motives while engaging in the same production and development tasks over a given period of time; the top manager of each was selected on the basis of his managerial style and was given instructions on how to run the organization.

Company *A* was designed to arouse the power motive. Set up along highly authoritarian lines, it left little room for individual initiative. All decisions were made by the president, jobs were well designed, and communication between positions was in writing. Company *B* was organized along democratic lines. The emphasis was on warm and friendly relationships rather than on task accomplishment or formal structures. Members were encouraged to talk and play. Daily group meetings were used to deal with interpersonal issues. The president was always available to his employees and encouraged them to bring their problems to him. Company C was designed to arouse the achievement motive. The president formulated objectives in collaboration with other executives, allowed groups to develop their own procedures, established a reward system for productivity, and constantly communicated his expectation of high performance by showing approval of good work. Although he was interested in everything that went on, he trusted others to make decisions affecting their own jobs. He posted progress reports for all to see whenever he received any data related to sales or new product acceptance.

To summarize some of their findings, job satisfaction was considerably higher in both the achievement- and affiliation-oriented climates (companies C and B) than in the power climate (company A). Company C (achievement) performed considerably better than either of the other two companies in terms of some relevant criteria. For example, it earned far more "profit" than either of the other two groups, it developed the greatest number of acceptable new products, and its overall performance was considerably better than that of the others. Research studies of this type dramatically demonstrate that behavior is a function of the person's motivational concern and of his perception of which of these concerns will be rewarded by the environment. The tendency to act in achievement-oriented ways, for example, does not necessarily mean that the individual has high achievement motivation. Management can stimulate achievement-oriented behavior (even from people who are not so motivated) by creating an achieving climate. Needless to say, this capacity to "manage" motivation has broad implications for the design and implementation of an MBO system.

Managing motivation in an organizational setting generally includes the consideration of the following key elements:

1) The latent needs of the individual (the subordinate).
2) The latent needs and leadership style of the manager (his supervisor).
3) The nature of the task to be performed.
4) The organizational climate or work environment.

The elements and the relationships between them are illustrated in

FIGURE 6–5. Key Elements in Managing Motivation. Source: Adapted from Kolb and Boyatzis, 1971, by permission of Prentice-Hall, Inc., Englewood Cliffs, New Jersey.

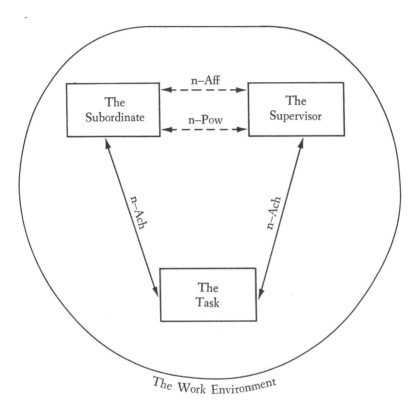

Figure 6–5. This model suggests that affiliative and power needs are directed at interpersonal relationships, while the need for achievement is directed at the task. The model further suggests that affiliative and power needs can be aroused both by association with other people and by the work environment. The need for achievement, on the other hand, can be aroused by the nature of the task as well as by the work environment. Although this deceptively simple model does not even begin to deal with all of the complexities of organizational life, it may help develop some additional insights into managing motivation via MBO.

The characteristics of most MBO systems are such that they tend to arouse the achievement motive in people. Achievement-oriented behavior is most likely to occur when the key elements identified in our model contain the following characteristics: [1]

1) The *subordinate* has a high need for achievement. As indicated earlier, he is eager to accept responsibility and to set high standards of performance for himself. He responds well to a challenging situation and tends to work better when confronted with a deadline or difficult task. He also likes to know how he is doing and tries to get specific feedback about his performance as soon and as often as he can.

2) His *supervisor* has a flexible leadership style and reinforces the achievement motive. He generally tends to maintain informality, encourages the acceptance of responsibility, stresses high standards of performance, and gives rewards and praise for a job well done. He stresses cooperation and provides support for the members of his team. He also encourages risk-taking and differences of opinion. He creates pride in the organization and stresses the fun and excitement of work.

3) The *task* is designed to arouse the need for achievement. The individual has a good deal of discretion or influence over what he does and how he does it. The task itself challenges his abilities and skills, contributes to the overall performance of the organization, and provides him with concrete feedback about the quality of his performance.

4) The *work environment* is also achievement-oriented. It emphasizes personal responsibility, encourages calculated risks and innovation, and provides for recognition and reward for good performance. A moderate (but not too high) degree of structure is provided in the form of policies, procedures, and rules. The achievement-oriented climate also provides for mutual support among members and creates the impression that the individual is a part of a successful team.

Given that latent motives and patterns of needs may differ among individuals, then the most effective managerial style in MBO is one which creates a task and work environment aimed at arousing

1. For descriptions of the characteristics of work tasks, climates, and leadership styles that tend to arouse the achievement, affiliation, and power motives, see Litwin and Stringer (1968, especially pp. 93–190).

and rewarding achievement-oriented behavior as described above. This generally requires collaborative problem-solving activities between and among levels of management. The role of the supervisor involves (1) providing an opportunity for individuals to become actively involved in creating work tasks which are significant in terms of organization goals and priorities, (2) helping them to establish challenging work objectives in their areas of responsibility, (3) assisting in the development of high standards of performance in the really important aspects of their jobs, (4) providing them with concrete and specific feedback about their performance, especially during periodic progress reviews, and (5) ensuring that the reward and penalty system is equitable—i.e., that good performance is rewarded. These activities are more likely to be successful when conducted in a climate that encourages mutual support, tolerates differences of opinion, and creates pride in being a member of a successful organization.

PARTICIPATION IN MBO SYSTEMS

The question of the nature and extent of participation in the MBO system is both important and controversial. At one extreme there are those who believe that top management should set goals and objectives and pass them down to lower levels of management. At the other, there are those who argue that lower levels of management should set the goals and hand them up to top management. The "top-down" and the "bottom-up" approaches, however, represent a faulty dichotomy. Neither extreme can be made to work effectively in the long run. While the overall aim of MBO is to increase participation in the management process at all levels of the organization, initially at least, it must be integrated with existing management philosophy and practices. Some organizations (and managers) can not readily adapt to an "ideal" system of managing by objectives. Consequently, the MBO system must be designed and implemented in a way which makes sense in terms of the existing organizational culture, values, and norms and gradually moves toward greater involvement and participation at all levels of management.

Rensis Likert (1961, 1967) provides some useful concepts and insights into the question of participation in the management of organizations. Drawing heavily from research done at the Institute for Social

Research, University of Michigan, Likert (1967) found a distinct pattern of participation in a number of prevailing management "systems."

System 1

Management is seen as having little or no confidence and trust in subordinates, who are seldom involved in decision-making and problem-solving. Most of the decisions are made at the top of the organization. Goal setting is also done at the top and distributed down through the chain of command. Motivation is stimulated primarily through fear and the threat of punishment, with only occasional rewards. What little interaction there is between levels of management generally takes place under conditions of fear and mistrust. The flow of communication is generally downward and tends to be viewed with suspicion at the lower levels. Upward communication, on the other hand, tends to be inaccurate. Managerial control is highly concentrated in the hands of top management and used in a policing or punitive manner.

System 2

Management is seen as having some confidence and trust in subordinates, though much in the condescending manner of the "master-slave" relationship. Policy is generally established at the top and many decisions are made at lower levels within a prescribed framework. Top management generally establishes goals and objectives, which may or may not be viewed with suspicion by lower levels. In terms of accuracy, only the information that the boss wants to hear flows upward. Other information is either restricted or filtered. There is a relatively high concentration of managerial control at the top with some delegation to the lower levels. Control data, coupled with rewards and punishments, are used at times to police operations or to guide activities in accordance with orders.

System 3

Although still wishing to maintain control over key decisions, management is seen as having substantial but not complete trust in subordinates. Top management establishes broad policies and makes general decisions. More specific decisions are made at the lower levels. Goals are established by higher management after a discussion of potential problems and planned actions with subordinates. Occasional punishment, reward, and some involvement are used to motivate behavior. There tends to be a moderate amount of interaction between levels of management, often with a fair amount of confidence and trust. Quite a bit of communication flows up and down the hierarchy. Some of it is at times viewed with suspicion and may or may not be questioned. There is a moderate delegation of the review and control processes to the lower levels of management. Control data are largely used for policing, with the emphasis usually on reward, but are also used to guide activities according to orders and sometimes for self-guidance.

System 4

Management is seen as having complete confidence and trust in subordinates. Decision-making is widely dispersed and well-integrated throughout the organization. Except in emergencies, goals are usually established through group participation. Motivation is based upon participation and involvement in setting goals, improving methods, appraising progress toward goals, and developing economic rewards. The interaction is extensive and friendly with a high degree of confidence and trust. There is a very substantial amount of cooperative teamwork present throughout the organization. There is a great deal of communication aimed at achieving organizational objectives between individuals and groups. Information flow is up, down, and across. It is generally accurate and accepted, but if not, openly and candidly questioned. The responsibility for review and control is quite widespread and delegated to lower levels of management. Control data are not used to police and punish. They are used primarily for self-guidance and for coordinating problem-solving.

To facilitate the analysis of organizational climate and environment, an instrument was developed to enable members to rate their organization in terms of its management system. The instrument is designed to collect data along such dimensions as leadership, motivation, communication flow and quality, decision-making, interaction and influence, goal setting, and the exercise of control by management. Hundreds of managers from many different organizations were asked to indicate where the *most* productive organization, division, or department they have known would fall along the above dimensions. These same managers were then asked to repeat the process and to indicate the *least* productive organization or subunit they have known. Likert found that those firms or plants which reflected System 4 characteristics showed high productivity, low scrap loss, low costs, favorable attitudes, and excellent labor relations. The opposite seemed to be the case for companies or departments whose management systems were close to System 1. Corresponding relationships were also found relative to any movement or shift from one management system toward the others. The movement of organizations toward System 4 was accompanied by long-range improvements in productivity and earnings, while the long-range consequences of movement toward System 1 were generally unfavorable.

According to Likert, System 4 management is based upon the use by the manager of the principle of supportive relationships, his use of his team for group decision-making, and his high performance goals for the organization. Supportive relationships are those which build and maintain a sense of personal worth and importance among individuals. The one-on-one relationship between a superior and a subordinate gives way to group interaction, with the superior providing a connecting link to the next higher level of management (those individuals who belong to more than one group are called "linking pins"). A mechanism is provided for participation in the goal-setting process through group decision-making and the linking function. As a consequence, established objectives represent the sound integration of individual needs and desires.

Likert's model describing the relative degree of participation in the management of an organization has some direct implications on the design and the implementation of a system of managing by objectives. The degree of participation in the MBO process, initially at least, must be consistent with current management philosophy, practice, and behavior. A participative approach to MBO will fail in a nonparticipative management system unless a major change effort is consciously planned and systematically implemented. Movement from System 1 toward System 4 management also involves changing the organization's culture, its values, its behavioral norms, and its way of doing things. There is no quick and easy solution to the problem. Major organizational changes generally require careful planning and a great deal of time for successful implementation. Although the MBO process can be designed to work in a variety of management systems, it tends to work best when there is active involvement and meaningful participation at all levels.

Perhaps most important, however, MBO can itself provide the vehicle for moving an organization toward System 4 management.

REFERENCES

Brayfield, A. H., and W. H. Crockett. "Employee attitudes and employee performance." *Psychological Bulletin* 52 (1955): 396–424.

Dunnette, M. D., J. P. Campbell, and M. D. Hakel. "Factors contributing to job satisfaction and job dissatisfaction in six occupational groups." *Organizational Behavior and Human Performance* 2 (May 1967): 143–174.

Georgopoulos, B. S., G. M. Mahoney, and N. W. Jones. "A path-goal approach to productivity." *Journal of Applied Psychology* 41 (1957): 345–53.

Herzberg, F. *Work and the Nature of Man.* World, 1966.

Herzberg, F., B. Mausner, and B. Snyderman. *The Motivation to Work.* Wiley, 1959.

House, R. J. "A path goal theory of leadership effectiveness." *Administrative Science Quarterly* 16 (Winter 1971): 321–38.

House, R. J., and L. A. Wigdor. "Herzberg's dual-factor theory of job satisfaction and motivation: A review of the evidence and a criticism." *Personnel Psychology* 20 (Winter 1967): 369–89.

Kolb, D. A., and R. E. Boyatzis. "On the dynamics of the helping relationship." In *Organizational Psychology: A Book of Readings,* D. A. Kolb, I. M. Rubin, and J. M. McIntyre, eds., pp. 339–55. Prentice-Hall, 1971.

Krech, D., and R. S. Crutchfield. *Elements of Psychology.* Knopf, 1958.

Likert, R. *New Patterns of Management.* McGraw-Hill, 1961.

Likert, R. *The Human Organization.* McGraw-Hill, 1967.

Litwin, G. H., and R. A. Stringer, Jr. *Motivation and Organization Climate.* Division of Research, Graduate School of Business Administration, Harvard University, 1968.

McClelland, D. C. *The Achieving Society.* Van Nostrand, 1961.

McGregor, D. M. *The Human Side of Enterprise.* McGraw-Hill, 1960.

Maslow, A. H. *Motivation and Personality.* Harper & Row, 1954.

Vroom, V. H. *Work and Motivation.* Wiley, 1964.

Review and Appraisal

THE NEED FOR PERFORMANCE APPRAISAL

The evaluation of organizational and individual performance is a necessary and integral part of the managerial role. Organizations are evaluated in many different ways by many different people. Customers and clients evaluate them on the basis of the relative quality of their products or services. Shareholders evaluate them in terms of earnings per share and the market price of their stock. Employees evaluate them according to the amount of extrinsic and intrinsic satisfaction derived from the work environment. In most cases, the criteria used by management to evaluate the performance of organizations and groups are clear and objective. Market penetration, sales volume, costs, profits, return on investment, productivity, scrap losses, turnover, and absenteeism represent only a few of the many available benchmarks.

The performance of individuals, on the other hand, is not so easily measured. The criteria are rarely clear or objective and frequently include such nebulous things as initiative, attitude, enthusiasm, judgment, and creativity. Despite the apparent problems of appraising individual performance, however, a great deal of time and effort go into the process. Why? There are several good reasons.

To begin with, the appraisal of an individual's performance is an essential element of motivation and control. Managerial control requires that activities and events be continuously evaluated in the light of planned behavior and results so that corrective action can be taken when required. This is also true of self-control, which requires that the individual monitor and correct his own behavior. The emphasis in either case is on improving present performance. Second, performance appraisal provides a basis for rewarding past performance and behavior. When tied to the organization's reward and penalty system, it can become an effective motivational tool. It can also be a motivating device when used to encourage individual growth and development. Third, the appraisal of individual performance provides much of the data required for manpower planning. For the organization, it can become the basis for a skills inventory or for identifying the training and development needs of its members. For the individual, it can become the basis for his career planning. Last, and perhaps most important of all, there are sound psychological reasons for evaluating an individual's performance. Each of us has a human need to learn, to grow, to develop our capabilities. This can only come about with appropriate feedback and a sense of accomplishment and progress. We also have an inherent need to "know where we stand" in terms of our competences and how our efforts are viewed by others. Individual performance appraisals help meet these psychological needs.

It may be useful at this point to distinguish between continuous appraisal and periodic evaluations. One is an ongoing and essential element in management, the other represents useful but discrete additions to the process. Continuous appraisal generally involves identifying and solving problems, giving advice and counsel, modifying tasks and assignments, reviewing and clarifying priorities, reassessing the nature and scope of delegated authority, and many other such activities designed to facilitate coordination and control. The continuous appraisal of individual performance is an integral part of the manager's job and is essential for effective management.

Unless supplemented by periodic evaluations, however, continuous appraisal may actually be dysfunctional. The heat of battle and the pressures of time may cause management to look past the man and focus on the work he is doing. The development of skills not required for the job at hand may be overlooked. There may be little if any "coaching" of the individual to help improve his present skills. There may be a tendency to focus on failures, to overlook successes, to deal only with weaknesses, to neglect strengths. There may be a lack of objectivity in the continuous appraisal process, so that there is a distinct need to step back and summarize performance at a given point in time. Periodic evaluations help minimize these dangers.

There is also a basic distinction between the more frequent progress reviews used to evaluate performance in MBO and the more conventional reviews used to appraise overall individual performance. Periodic MBO reviews are generally designed to solve problems, take corrective action, and measure progress toward specified objectives and targets. Rarely if ever do the objectives reflect an individual's (or a group's) *total* responsibilities. The individual review is intended to evaluate the individual's *overall* performance during a given time period.

THE PERIODIC MBO REVIEW:
APPRAISING PROGRESS

The periodic analysis and evaluation of performance is an integral part of any system of management by objectives. As indicated in Figure 7–1, the basic purpose of the periodic review is to evaluate individual or group progress toward established objectives. The focus of this seventh step in the MBO process is on problem-solving and corrective action. Periodic progress reviews also provide important inputs into the appraisal of overall individual performance. Depending upon whether the evaluation concerns the progress of an individual manager or that of a management team, the session itself may follow any one of several different formats.

Superior-subordinate reviews generally involve the individual and his immediate supervisor. These "one-on-one" sessions are used to systematically monitor progress toward the subordinate manager's objectives. Depending upon the quality of the relationship between them, the supervisor may play a number of different roles during the review. He may act as a teacher, a coach, or a consultant to the subordinate manager. He may serve as a sounding board, offer suggestions, give advice and counsel, and play an active role in helping solve the actual or potential problems confronting his subordinate. Because of his position, he frequently has the information or authority to make decisions the subordinate manager could not make on his own. The superior-subordinate review is used at all levels of management and is perhaps the most popular format in use today.

Committee reviews generally involve the manager, his immediate supervisor, and a number of other interested parties. These individuals may be members of various staff departments or higher levels

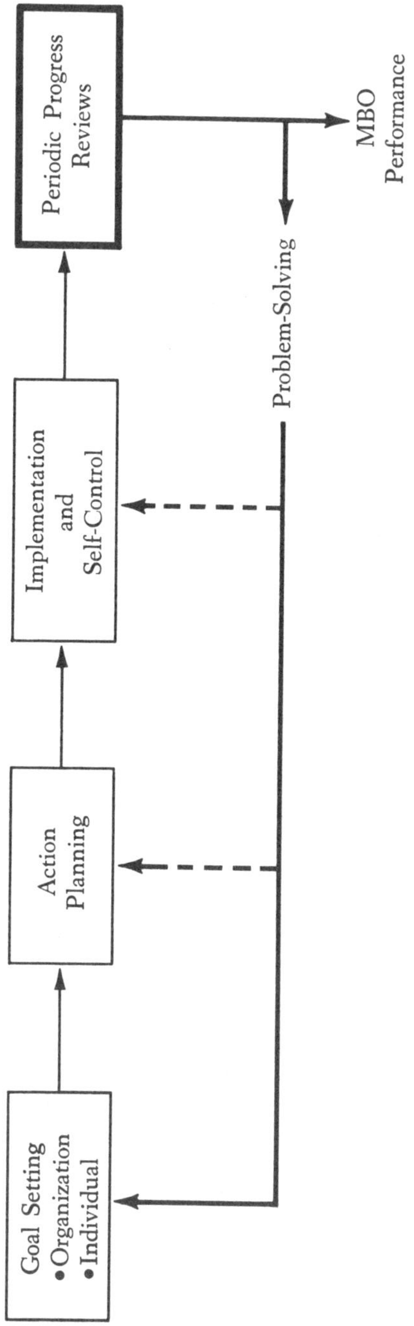

FIGURE 7–1. MBO as a System: Step 7.

of management. As in the case above, the group acts as a monitor and resource pool. The additional members usually possess specific knowledge or skills required to help solve some of the problems confronting the manager. In some cases, they possess the combined authority to resolve technical or managerial issues that cut across organization lines. The use of committees to review individual performance is generally reserved for middle and upper levels of management.

Management team reviews generally involve a work group consisting of the manager and his subordinates. The review is aimed at measuring the progress of the management team toward its goals and objectives. While the above formats are intended to monitor the performance of an *individual,* the team review is designed to monitor the performance of a *group.* The members of the management team share ownership and responsibility for a common set of objectives and work together toward their attainment. They monitor their own progress and serve as a collective pool of resources. The focus is generally on joint problem-solving and improving work relationships. The team review can be used at almost any level in the organization where it is possible to establish meaningful objectives for a work group. To be successful, however, the approach must be consistent with the management philosophy and style of the manager of the team.

Periodic progress reviews are necessary to effective management by objectives. They provide essential feedback to the relevant parties and close the loop between planned performance and actual results. In general, they serve as a vehicle for the following functions in the MBO process:

1) *Remove obstacles.* There are instances when the manager will not be able to meet his objectives because of obstacles which he cannot deal with himself. In many cases, the obstacle or cause of a problem has been identified by him *prior* to the review and he has already outlined a course of action designed to enable him to reach his stated objectives. He may simply need the approval of higher authority, his boss or the review group, to take the necessary action. Or he may want to "reality test" his solution to assess its impact on other departments or managers in the organization.

2) *Identify problems.* There may also be instances where the manager has not identified the cause of the problem he is facing. All he knows is that he will not be able to meet his objectives. In this case, the periodic review provides an oppor-

tunity to combine data and talents to help him identify actual and potential problems. By combining his own information and expertise with his boss (or the review group), he has a better chance to distinguish between symptoms and causes. Two or more heads are often better than one.

3) *Solve problems.* Once a problem has been identified, whether prior to or during the review, realistic alternative solutions must be developed and evaluated before an appropriate course of action can be formulated. As already indicated, two or more heads are often desirable. This is especially true if the planned solution involves coordination with other parties. It is also possible to decide during the review *not* to solve a particular problem. Other problems may be more pressing, it may be too costly to resolve, or it may be easier to live with the problem than to resolve it at this time.

4) *Plan for and take corrective action.* As indicated in Figure 7-1, corrective action can take a number of paths. It may involve a change in the way the action plan is being implemented by the manager. Or it may involve changing the action plan itself. The changes may be dictated by problems and obstacles, as discussed above, or by changing conditions or priorities.

5) *Revise existing objectives.* Corrective action may also include revising one or more of the stated objectives. The change may involve an increase or a decrease in the level of some of the objectives, schedule modifications, or a rearrangement of their relative priorities. It may also involve dropping an objective which is no longer appropriate in the light of additional data.

6) *Establish new objectives.* In some instances, changing conditions and priorities may make it advisable to add one or more objectives to the list. These may be in the same or different result areas, may be aimed at solving a particular problem, or may be the result of a new opportunity or innovative idea which has surfaced. The establishment of a new set of objectives becomes one of the primary functions of the periodic review scheduled at the end of the goal-setting time period (e.g., the end of the fiscal or calendar year).

7) *Review performance.* Periodic MBO reviews also provide an opportunity to review performance. Individual or group performance can be assessed and suggestions can be made for

improvement. Depending upon their frequency, periodic reviews also provide more timely feedback to everyone concerned. In this sense, they facilitate the process of continuous
appraisal. Perhaps most important, however, they provide significant inputs into the overall evaluation of an individual's
performance.

There are many questions concerning the nature and role of
periodic progress reviews in management by objectives. What type of
reviews should they be? Who should participate? When and where
are they held? How long should they last? How often are they conducted? The answers, of course, depend upon such things as the nature
of the environment, the period of time covered by the objectives and
action plans, and the geographic locations of the departments and individuals. Some general observations may, however, be made about the
nature and use of MBO progress reviews.

Management team reviews

Management team reviews are generally used when dealing
with the overall goals, strategic plans, and performance objectives of an
organization or group. They are generally most effective at the upper
levels of management where there is shared ownership and responsibility for the overall performance of the unit. A brief description of
how one company uses the team review may shed some light on the
questions raised above. The corporation owns and operates five theme
amusement parks around the country.

Participants • Members of the top management team participate in the review. They include the executive vice-president (who
is the chief corporate officer), the four corporate staff vice-presidents
(marketing, show productions, finance, and administration), and the
general managers of the parks.

Frequency • Given the seasonal nature of the business, the
MBO reviews are scheduled to take place during the "off season" and
are conducted three times a year.

Purpose • The nature and role of the review tends to vary.
In September, for example, the focus is on reviewing past performance
and problem-solving, but some attention is also paid to determining
priorities for the coming year. The focus of the December meeting is

on goal setting and action planning. This includes modifying the five-year corporate plan and the three-year park plans, as well as developing overall performance objectives for the corporation and for the individual parks. The March meeting is generally aimed at rearranging priorities, problem-solving, and finalizing overall performance objectives and action plans for the year.

Time and place • The three-day sessions are generally conducted away from the normal place of business. The December review is held near the corporate office, while the other reviews are rotated to off-site locations near the various parks.

Other reviews • Although the process tends to vary from park to park, team reviews are also conducted by the individual park managers and include the members of his top management team. These are generally held in the fall and are concerned with reviewing past performance and developing overall park objectives for the coming year. It should be noted here that superior-subordinate reviews are conducted annually (on a one-on-one basis) to appraise the performance of lower-level managers in the parks and corporate offices.

Committee reviews

As indicated above, committee reviews generally involve the manager of a major organizational unit or product line, one or more people from higher levels of management, and other interested parties. Committee MBO reviews tend to have a problem-solving focus, as illustrated by the following description. In this case, we will describe the use of this form of review by a large industrial manufacturer with some sixteen plants geographically dispersed throughout the United States and Canada.

Participants • In addition to the individual plant manager, members of the reviewing committee include the director of production, the vice-president of manufacturing, and several representatives from the staff and service departments (e.g., quality control, industrial engineering, budgeting, etc.).

Frequency • The reviews are conducted quarterly in March, June, September, and December.

Purpose • Given that the company operates on a fiscal year basis, the nature and focus of the reviews tend to vary. The emphasis of the June review, for example, is on appraising overall plant performance for the past fiscal year and presenting plant objectives for the coming year. The September, December, and March reviews are essentially to review progress and to identify and solve problems.

Time and place • The meetings are alternately held at the corporate offices and at the individual plants. In June and December, for example, the plant managers visit the home office for two or three days. This provides them with an opportunity to conduct other business with the staff and service departments on a face-to-face basis. The March and September meetings are conducted at each plant. The MBO reviews generally take about one day, depending upon the problems, and other subjects or activities are scheduled during the visit by the review team.

Other reviews • MBO reviews are conducted more frequently at the plant level. Depending upon the size of the plant, management team reviews are held monthly to appraise progress and to solve problems. Participants generally include the plant manager and his key supervisors. More frequent meetings are conducted by supervisors with the foremen at the lower levels. These are generally focused on production and scheduling problems.

Superior-subordinate reviews

The superior-subordinate review is perhaps the most common format used in most MBO systems. While management team and committee reviews tend to be used when the emphasis is on overall organizational or group objectives, or when an individual is held responsible for the objectives of his unit, one-on-one reviews tend to be used when the emphasis is on individual job objectives. As in the other cases, the focus tends to be on problem-solving. The answers to the specific questions raised above tend to vary from situation to situation.

Participants • The subordinate and his immediate supervisor generally participate in the review.

Frequency • The number of formally scheduled reviews tends to vary within and between organizations. More than one review is generally held during the time period covered by the objectives and action plans. In one company, for example, superior-subordinate reviews are conducted biweekly at the foreman level because of rapidly changing priorities and the use of three shifts.

Purpose • Depending upon the frequency of the review, the nature and purpose of the meeting is to monitor progress and solve problems. They may also be used to revise objectives and priorities or to establish new job objectives, but it is perhaps more important that they tend to facilitate vertical communications between the various levels of management.

Time and place • They are generally scheduled in the supervisor's office and may last anywhere from two to four hours.

Other reviews • As indicated above, superior-subordinate reviews may be used to supplement management team and committee reviews. In any event, they provide an important input into the performance appraisal process.

In summary, then, periodic progress reviews are an essential element in the MBO process. They can deal with either individual or group performance relative to stated objectives and expected results. The focus in either case is on problem-solving and taking corrective action if required. They are also an integral part of the continuous process of appraising an individual's performance. Periodic reviews can be held weekly, monthly, quarterly, semiannually, or even annually. Their frequency depends upon conditions and the needs of the organization. They tend to be held more frequently at lower levels of the organization and less frequently at higher levels. They also tend to be held more frequently in a dynamic and changing environment. Periodic reviews can facilitate vertical and horizontal communication throughout the organization. They are most effective when there is a free and open flow of ideas and a climate of collaboration and mutual trust between the participants.

THE INDIVIDUAL REVIEW: APPRAISING OVERALL PERFORMANCE

The need for appraising individual performance in organizations has already been noted. Although formal performance appraisal systems are of relatively recent origin, the evaluation of one man's work by another is not new. Supervisors have always evaluated their subordinates. While it is no doubt true that the evaluations may have been made in a random and slipshod manner, frequently unsupported and unrecorded, they have always been important to personnel actions. The changes that have come with formal performance appraisal systems are not a matter of making evaluations where none existed before. They involve rather a shift from random evaluations to the more systematic

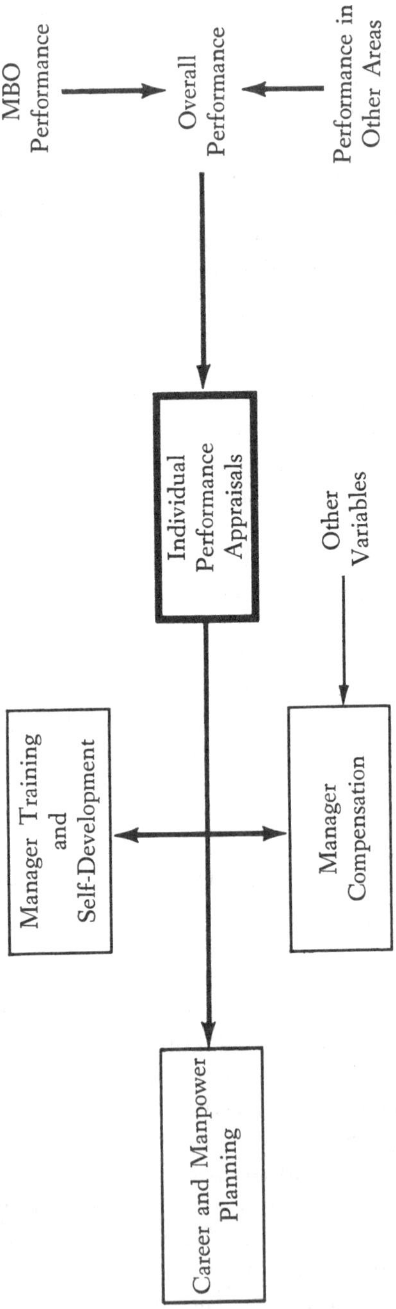

FIGURE 7–2. MBO as a System: Step 8.

appraisal of performance as an ongoing activity. The question, then, is not whether management should evaluate individual performance. The real issue is whether or not the process meets the needs of both the individual and the organization. This section deals with some of the key questions and considerations in appraising overall performance. More specifically, what kinds of performance should be evaluated? How can this be done most effectively? What are some of the potential dangers of appraisal systems? How can they be avoided?

Major factors of performance and potential

As indicated in Figure 7–2, individual performance reviews are an integral part of any MBO system. They involve an appraisal of current *performance* and an assessment of future *potential*. In turn, these provide a basis for management development, manager compensation, and career planning for the individual. The appraisal of present accomplishments and results is based upon the individual's overall performance. This includes not only his accomplishments in terms of specified objectives, but his performance in other areas as well. The assessment of future potential, on the other hand, includes both the individual's personal characteristics and his potential for advancement. Thus, there are at least four major ingredients that should be considered in individual performance reviews.

MBO performance • Measurable results and tangible accomplishments can provide a solid foundation for evaluating an individual's contribution to an organization. Clearly stated and verifiable objectives also provide the basis for useful standards and criteria. While the appraisal of performance in terms of specified results represents a tremendous improvement in traditional appraisal systems, there are a number of reasons why MBO performance should not be the *only* input into the process. First, the attainment of a given objective may sometimes be the result of circumstances beyond the manager's control. Luck or misfortune frequently have a hand in what is actually achieved. Second, given the nature and complexity of most managerial jobs, it is virtually impossible to define them entirely in tangible and verifiable terms. There are many aspects and activities which defy measurement and quantification. Third, the focus is on accomplishments and results. MBO does not provide a way of accurately assessing management methods and processes. Fourth, the emphasis tends to be on performance in a job which is presently held. Effective manpower planning also requires the identification and appraisal of *potential* to ensure that the future needs of both the individual and the organization are met. Fifth, and perhaps most important, MBO tends to emphasize short-run performance and results. Care must be taken to evaluate the long-term implications of present accomplishments.

Performance as a manager • Given the above limitations, especially the potential danger of overemphasizing short-term results, the individual's performance and accomplishments as a manager should also be included in the appraisal. This generally involves planning the use of resources, organizing and delegating the work, motivating and developing subordinates, and monitoring activities and events to ensure the attainment of organizational goals. A number of useful guidelines and schemes have been developed to facilitate the appraisal of managerial performance (see Koontz, 1971). Although they should be tailor-made for a given organization or level of management, they generally evolve around key management processes and techniques.

Planning includes the ability to identify opportunities, analyze problems, establish priorities and needs, and allocate available resources. This also includes the establishment of policies and procedures, objectives and standards of performance, forecasts and budgets, and programs and schedules.

Organizing and staffing includes the ability to delegate and coordinate the work required to meet objectives within specified time and budget limits, to provide qualified personnel to meet organizational goals, and to plan for managerial progression.

Motivating and developing includes the ability to utilize the skills and abilities of subordinates, to establish and maintain a high degree of esprit among them, to encourage and provide for their self-development, and to broaden and strengthen their job-related capabilities.

Reviewing and monitoring includes the ability to review and measure progress against specified criteria, to take appropriate corrective action as necessary, and to evaluate and improve performance.

Personal qualifications and characteristics • In addition to evaluating performance, the appraisal process should also provide a basis for assessing the future potential of an individual. Some of the more important considerations involve his personal qualifications and characteristics. Personal qualifications essentially include factors related to educational background and work experience. Most of the factors can be easily verified and made a part of the man's record. Personal characteristics, on the other hand, might include personality traits, level

of intelligence, occupational interests, and any number of specific apti-
tudes or skills deemed necessary for promotions to higher levels of
responsibility. Although these are somewhat more difficult to measure
or verify, there are a number of tests which, when combined with
other data, may be of some help in assessing potential.

   Potential for advancement • In addition to personal qualifications and characteristics, the assessment of future potential involves
a number of other considerations and factors. These generally center
around the career goals of the individual and the manpower needs of
the organization. The manager's interests and desires, his general health,
his family situation, his willingness to move, and many other factors
determine if he is *available* and *suitable* for advancement. His actual
promotion or advancement to another position depends upon the present
and future needs of the organization, the suitability and availability of
other candidates, and any number of other external factors.

   In summary, then, the appraisal process involves an assessment
of both performance and potential. Although MBO-related activities
and results provide important inputs, the individual's accomplishments
as a manager must also be considered when appraising overall present
performance. The assessment of future potential involves relating personal data and career goals to the present and future manpower needs
of the organization. Each of the ingredients provides an important input
and is an essential element of the appraisal system. One should not be
emphasized at the expense of the other. They should be treated in a
balanced way. If this cannot be accomplished during the same review,
it may be better to deal with the question of potential in a separate
meeting.

PROBLEMS AND ISSUES

   Appraising performance is an extremely difficult chore for most
managers. It is hard for most of us to pass judgment on someone else,
particularly if it is to become part of the record and affect his future
with the organization. Yet there is a need to measure, compare, and
record performance if organizational goals and objectives are to be
achieved. And if growth is to occur, it becomes necessary to evaluate
potential. While a system of managing by objectives can provide much
of the objective data required for a formal appraisal system, there are

a number of problems and issues which remain. For example, what is the impact of feedback on performance? Who should rate the individual's performance? What skills, if any, are required to conduct a performance review? Should the review also deal with salary and promotion? An attempt to deal with some of these questions and issues follows.[1]

The impact of feedback

The use of specific, concrete feedback, if properly done, can be an effective tool for motivating and developing people. Ideally, the performance appraisal session should be goal oriented, should have a problem-solving focus, and should be conducted by a skilled reviewer. Some of the studies conducted at General Electric during the mid-sixties [2] seem to provide some appropriate guidelines. In general, they indicate that:

1) Performance tends to improve when specific objectives are established for the job.

2) The participation of a subordinate in setting his own performance objectives yields favorable results.

3) Mutual goal setting by the superior and the subordinate produces positive results.

4) Criticism tends to have a negative impact on the attainment of objectives. As a consequence, defensiveness can result in inferior performance.

5) Praise has little, if any, effect on the achievement of goals.

6) Coaching is best done on a day-to-day basis when related to specific behavior and results, not once a year.

7) Interviews intended primarily to improve performance should not at the same time deal with salary and promotion.

8) Separate performance evaluations are generally required for different purposes.

1. For one review of management appraisal practices, see Miner, 1968.
2. See, for example, Meyer, Kay, and French (1965).

Superior, peer, subordinate, and self-ratings

Most appraisal systems and forms are designed to be completed by the immediate supervisor. A few, however, may involve peers, subordinates, or the individual himself. There is some evidence that self-interest can influence peer, subordinate, and self-ratings to the point where they differ considerably from the ratings given by superiors. Self-ratings, for example, tend to emphasize getting along with others as important for success, while superiors tend to stress such things as job knowledge and initiative. Peers also seem to consider somewhat different factors.

Despite these differences, additional inputs to the appraisal process have some potential advantages. The General Electric studies suggest that participation in setting job objectives and appraising performance can contribute to more effective performance. This kind of self-rating has at least some value in management development. There is also some evidence that it is possible to get objective and useful peer evaluations at the middle and upper levels of management. Peer evaluations may be particularly valuable for identifying leadership potential.

Miner (1968) suggests that tripartite approaches, consisting of superior, peer, and self-ratings, will provide the basis for future management appraisal systems. There are numerous advantages. The biases contained in peer and self-ratings will be reduced when it is known that ratings by the superior are also obtained. The inputs from these different sources provide an integrated, composite view of the individual's performance, his development, and his potential. To the extent that the ratings are consistent, acceptance of the evaluation and subsequent personnel actions are more likely to be supported. Differences, on the other hand, may help identify problems and biases in the process. Important considerations may be lost if only ratings by the superior are obtained. Unfortunately, however, most organizations lack expertise to develop and effectively utilize tripartite appraisal systems.

Primacy versus recency

There is evidence that initial impressions (primacy) and recent events (recency) tend unduly to affect performance appraisal. The "halo effect" is a well-known illustration of the problem of primacy. Other studies, however, indicate that specific instances of behavior or events occurring shortly before the review can also bias the evaluation. Some raters apparently remember recent events more vividly and as a result tend to weigh them more heavily.

The problems created by these phenomena suggest the importance of continuous or relatively frequent appraisals. They also suggest the need for documentation in the evaluation process. Periodic MBO progress reviews can help minimize both types of biases.

The skill of the rater

This is perhaps the most crucial element in the performance appraisal process. Poorly conducted reviews and evaluations can undermine the entire MBO program. Successful progress reviews and performance appraisals rest heavily on the ability to act in a consultative rather than a judgmental manner. Problem-solving and learning are at the heart of the process. Proper training in consultative skills and interpersonal communications, including the ability to provide feedback in a constructive manner, can go a long way toward improving a manager's ability to review progress and appraise performance.

Performance appraisals versus salary reviews

With respect to motivation and development, the General Electric studies also indicate that it is undesirable to deal with salary recommendations and promotions during the performance review. When criticism is tied directly to pay actions, defensiveness on the part of the person being rated tends to block any learning. His energies tend to be focused on self-protection rather than self-improvement.

Separating performance appraisals from salary recommendations is one way to reduce the distortions. The real solution, however, may be to provide the kind of training that will help managers avoid the tendency to decide first on the salary actions and then to adjust the performance ratings to match. As we shall discuss in the next chapter, performance is not the only factor which influences merit increases.

GUIDELINES AND ILLUSTRATIONS

As indicated earlier, the appraisal of performance is a continuous activity. Periodic evaluations are, however, required to provide form and substance in the process. Progress reviews are an essential element of managing by objectives. They provide a systematic way for mutual definition and establishment of objectives, refinement of action plans, equation of accomplishments to expected results, and analysis and improvement of current performance. Overall performance reviews, on the other hand, provide additional opportunities to evaluate an individual's *total* performance and to assess his future potential. MBO progress reviews tend to be conducted more frequently and provide a significant input into the more formal individual performance reviews. There is a wide variety of possible combinations and approaches, depending upon the organization and its management philosophy. Many organizations simply combine the two types of reviews into one annual or semiannual conference between the supervisor and his subordinate manager. Regardless of the format, however, they all involve the following key elements in one form or another:

1) A set of mutually agreed-upon objectives and expected results. These are generally the result of meaningful interaction between the relevant parties.

2) An analysis of the subordinate manager's progress and performance relative to the previously established objectives. The intent is to resolve potential problems and to identify his specific accomplishments.

3) An appraisal of his overall performance to identify the needs and opportunities to develop his present job-related skills. Although the appraisal may eventually result in some sort of "rating," or comparison of the individual to other managers, its purpose is to improve present performance and to develop future potential. The appraisal also provides a basis for evaluating his *total* performance and the more long-range effects of his efforts to accomplish current objectives and targets.

4) An agreement on job-related and development objectives for the next appraisal period. This generally involves a reassessment of organizational goals and priorities.

5) The formulation of action plans which will result in the development of the manager in his present job. Some attention may also be paid to developing his future potential.

The actual preparation for and conduct of the performance review depends largely upon the managerial styles of and the quality of the relationship between the supervisor and his subordinate manager. It is not something that one person (the boss) does to another person (the subordinate). Ideally, it is a collaborative process in which both participants are actually and meaningfully involved. Preparation for the formal meeting or conference goes on during the entire review period—that is, from the end of the last conference to the beginning of the next one. A number of useful guidelines have been developed to facilitate the process:

1) *Strive for objectivity.* Performance and accomplishments should be evaluated in terms which are tangible, or at least verifiable. Note and consider the existence of any "extenuating circumstances."

2) *Focus on observed behavior.* Performance should be based upon observable behavior. Get complete and factual information. The act of "observing" should be active, continuous, and purposeful.

3) *Look for significant incidents.* The analysis of performance should be based upon specific incidents or events which provide valid insights into work behavior.

4) *Record the observations.* A way of recording observations as they are made should be devised and used. This provides a source of accurate data to supplement the appraisal process.

5) *Recognize joint responsibility.* The impact of the supervisor's behavior on the manager's efforts to get results must be considered. The supervisor should make his observations complete by considering the impact of his own behavior on the performance of his subordinate.

6) *Provide for feedback.* Timely and appropriate feedback to the individual provides a solid foundation for improved performance. Remember, the best way to develop subordinates is to coach them on a day-to-day basis.

The conference itself may be conducted in any number of different ways. Again, the exact format and process depend upon personal styles and the relationship between the participants. It is *not* an activity in which one person sits in judgment on the other. It is more accurately a "helping" activity in which one person guides, counsels, and supports another. Several general considerations have been developed to guide managers through the various phases of the performance review:

1) *Focus on accomplishments and results.* Normally, the first part of the discussion deals with performance in terms of specified objectives. The focus is on expected results, the ways

in which performance is measured, and the actual accomplishments and contributions of the subordinate manager. There should be a free flow of information between the participants. Various approaches and techniques can be used to initiate and conduct the discussion. It is the supervisor's responsibility, however, to provide direction and guide the discussion so that definite conclusions can be reached.

2) *Discuss total performance.* There should next be a discussion of the individual's overall performance. This might include, among other things, an appraisal of his other managerial activities and the more long-range impact of his current efforts. Subjectivity can be minimized by providing complete information and by describing specific incidents or events. The accuracy and availability of these data depend upon the amount of preparation and documentation that preceded the meeting. The roles and responsibilities of the participants are essentially the same during this phase of the discussion as they were earlier.

3) *Formulate development plans.* Since the conference is generally concerned with the performance and development of the subordinate, it is suggested that he take a more active role during this phase of the discussion. Normally, he has come prepared to discuss *his* job and *his* self-development plan. The supervisor's role at this point should be one of coaching and actually supporting the manager. Although some opportunities for development exist "outside" of the job, most management development occurs through "on-the-job" opportunities and performance.

4) *Discuss the future.* Unless it is to be covered at another meeting or conference, the final phase of the discussion should cover the manager's career aspirations and plans. These must be *realistically* discussed in the context of the organization's present and future manpower needs. There may or may not be enough information available at the time. Consequently, it may sometimes be necessary to gather more information and to schedule another meeting for the express purpose of formulating a concrete career plan for the individual.

5) *Document the conclusions.* Although documentation should not be one of the main activities performed during a performance review, it is essential that a record be kept of the conclusions and results of the meeting. A variety of forms have been developed to facilitate the process. Copies that are

retained by the participants provide each of them with a record of their mutual understanding and become the basis for subsequent reviews. Equally as important, however, they can become part of an organization's information system and can play a significant role in manpower planning.

Although the use of forms is not essential to managing by objectives and appraising individual performance, they can facilitate the process and do provide documentation for future reference. A typical example might be composed of five parts, one of which is designed to appraise the manager's MBO performance. It deals with specific accomplishments and results in major result areas and pays specific attention to work relationships and self-development activities. The second part is concerned with appraising his performance as a manager with emphasis on the methods and techniques used to achieve the objectives and to manage his overall area of responsibility. Personal qualifications and characteristics are covered in the third part, along with information concerning health and appearance. The fourth provides for a general summary of the appraisal and identifies areas and methods which might be improved. The discussion around the first four parts is usually done in a coaching or counseling mode in the context of developing new commitments for the coming period. The last part calls for the supervisor's judgments concerning the individual's potential for advancement and the positions for which he might be considered in the future. Unless he were actually under consideration for promotion, the supervisor would probably not discuss these judgments with the subordinate manager.

REFERENCES

Koontz, H. *Appraising Managers as Managers.* McGraw-Hill, 1971.

Meyer, H. H., E. Kay, and J. P. R. French. "Split roles in performance appraisal." *Harvard Business Review* 43 (January-February 1965): 123–29.

Miner, J. B. "Management appraisal: A capsule review and current references." *Business Horizons* 11 (October 1968): 83–96.

Key Relationships

8

MANAGER TRAINING
AND SELF-DEVELOPMENT

We have already stressed the importance of integrating management by objectives with key organizational processes. Market forecasts, data processing, budgets, and the like must be properly tied to the MBO system if it is to become a natural way of managing in the organization. Integration is further strengthened through management development, compensation, and career and manpower planning. As illustrated in Figure 8-1, these are important elements of an MBO system. Each is a by-product of the performance appraisal process, and each is necessary to reinforce desired behavior and to strengthen motivation. MBO is most effective when it provides for individual growth and development, when behavior and performance are clearly linked to organization rewards and penalties, and when it provides for the present and future manpower needs of the organization. This chapter is devoted to exploring these key relationships in greater detail.

It may be helpful to distinguish at the outset between "manager training" and "manager development." Manager training generally refers to specific programs or courses offered to provide an individual with an opportunity to learn the knowledge, skills, and attitudes needed to be a successful manager. Manager development, on the other hand, refers to the progress he actually makes in learning how to manage. The former is concerned with creating the environment and an oppor-

FIGURE 8–1.   MBO as a System: Steps 8a, 8b, and 8c.

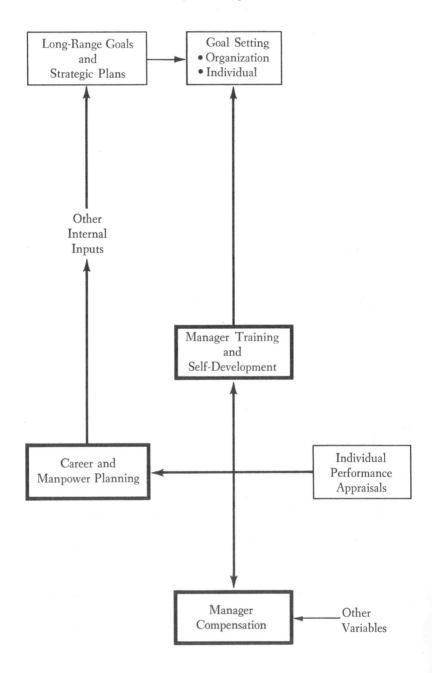

The self-development process, graphically illustrated in Figure 8–2, includes the following four major elements:

1) *A diagnosis of training and development needs.* This important first step begins with an identification of the present and future requirements of the job. What are the knowledge, skills, and attitudes required to be effective in my present job? What will they need to be in the future? The information required to answer these questions may come from several sources, including the manager's experience and discussions with his supervisor and with other managers. The diagnosis also involves an honest assessment of present abilities and levels of competence. What are my major strengths and weaknesses? What knowledge, skills, and attitudes do I presently have? How do they fit in with the requirements of the job? The answers to questions such as these generally come from a realistic self-appraisal and appropriate feedback from others. In general, the self-assessment process should lead to the identification of specific gaps in the knowledge, skills, and attitudes required for the job.

2) *The establishment of goals and objectives.* A second element is setting self-development goals. These are generally based upon an assessment of priorities and the availability of resources. Since the manager can not meet all of his development needs at the same time, he must identify and deal with those which are most important. What are the differences (gaps) between the present level of each specific knowledge or skill and the requirements of the job? How significant are the gaps? Which are most important to the present job? Which will be most important in the future? The availability of resources is closely related to the question of priorities. Which needs can best be met through on-the-job training? What are the best ways to acquire the needed knowledge, skills, and attitudes? Are there any in-house resources available or should the needs be met through external programs and courses? Once the manager's self-development goals have been established, they can become the basis for his specific personal growth and development objectives and an integral part of the MBO system.

3) *The development of action plans.* The third element of the process is formulating a concrete plan or program for self-development. This generally involves specifying how the ob-

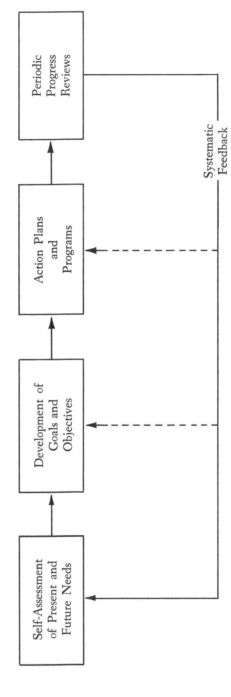

FIGURE 8–2.   The Self-Development Process.

jectives will be met within the desired schedules. Needless to say, the program must be practical in terms of the real needs of both the individual and the organization.

4) *The review of progress.* A final element is the systematic review of progress in terms of training and development needs. The manager receives feedback as part of the performance appraisal process and, as required, either takes corrective action or develops a new set of objectives and action plans.

The resources for self-development are all around the manager. There are many books and professional journals available to him. A wide variety of courses and programs are offered to broaden his knowledge and to help him improve his management skills. Numerous conferences, seminars, and workshops are conducted or sponsored by the company he works for. And his own on-the-job experiences can be converted into learning opportunities by building into them the means for appropriate feedback and analysis. Although there is no one best way to do it, the individual manager can and should facilitate his own growth and development.

An illustration

The manager should consider the following steps when planning a program of self-development:

Step 1 • The manager should identify the specific knowledge and skills required for each of the relevant areas of his job. Although the requirements may tend to vary from person to person, they may be placed in the general categories of:

1) *Knowledge of the environment.* The manager generally requires a good understanding of some of the factors in the *external* environment. Depending upon his job, for example, he may need to know the intricacies of the market place, the characteristics of the customers, the nature of the industry and competitors, the sources of supply, or government regulations and procedures. He also needs to understand the management philosophy and practices, organizational goals, objectives, structure, policies, and procedures, and a wide variety of other factors related to the *internal* environment.

2) *Technical competence.* Despite the notion that management is a universal skill, the manager must have at least some

understanding of the technical aspects of the work being managed. The managers of scientists and engineers, for example, must be acquainted with the specialized function or discipline they are managing. *The manager must know his business.* Without technical skill, he may be out of touch with the real problems of his organization. He may find it difficult to communicate with the people with whom he works, and, perhaps more important, he may be hard pressed to appraise their performance accurately.

3) *Management tools and techniques.* An understanding of the general body of knowledge related to the theory and practice of management is essential. There are a number of relevant and useful "principles" which can help guide the manager and make him more effective. Knowledge of and the ability to use a variety of tools and techniques, such as forecasting and budgeting, can facilitate the planning process. More effective decisions can result from model building, simulation, and a wide range of other quantitative techniques. A better understanding of personality theory and human motivation can facilitate selecting and training human resources. The manager who has a good grasp of the basic concepts and tools of management can influence his environment. One who does not, however, is forced to operate on a trial and error basis.

4) *Analytical ability.* A manager must have the skill to analyze and solve complex problems. He must be able to apply his analytical tools systematically and creatively; to identify the key issues; to deal with causes rather than symptoms; and, when the problems are solved, to translate the solutions into action. The manager must also have the ability to see the organization as a whole. This includes recognizing how its key functions and elements relate to one another and how changes in any one affect all of the others. It also includes visualizing the relationship of his organization to other organizations, to the community, and to society as a whole.

5) *Human skill.* Since management involves working with people, either as a leader of the team or as a group member, human skill is perhaps the most essential of all management skills, at every level of the organization. The primary tool of this skill is interpersonal communication. The manager must be able to communicate with many unique individuals and groups whose perceptions of the situation may differ. The skillful manager is both sensitive and flexible. He is aware of his

own perceptions and attitudes, as well as his feelings and needs. He is sensitive to the unique needs and motivations of other people and can understand their points of view. Having this sensitivity, he is then able and willing to act in an appropriate way.

The above skills reflect the ability of the manager to translate knowledge into action. They are so interrelated that it is difficult to distinguish between them. Although all are important management skills, their relative importance depends upon circumstances. For example, at higher levels of management technical skill becomes less and less important. The top executive may require little technical expertise if he has competent subordinates and if he possesses a high degree of the other management skills. Analytical skill, on the other hand, becomes increasingly more important at higher levels of management. The ability of the top executive to conceptualize and analyze complex problems is directly related to the success of his organization. Human skill, however, is important at every level and tends to vary with the number and frequency of personal contacts.

Step 2 • The manager should list the specific knowledges and skills which have any importance for his job, perhaps in column 1 of a self-assessment form similar to the one shown as Figure 8–3.

FIGURE 8–3. A Self-Assessment Form.

Name Specific Management Knowledge and Skills Col. 1	Importance to the Job Col. 2		Present Level of Knowledge or Skill Col. 3	Gaps Col. 4	
	Now	Future		Now	Future

Step 3 • He should indicate the relative importance of each item on the list to his job *now* and its anticipated importance in the *future*, rating each item from 1, of some importance, to 5, essential, and writing the two numbers in the two spaces provided in column 2 of the form.

Step 4 • He should assess his current level of competence, knowledge, or skill through self-analysis and feedback from others. He should then rate himself from 1, poor, to 5, thorough, and mark his response in column 3.

Step 5 • He should identify and rank the significant "gaps" between his present level of knowledge or skill in each area and its importance to his job *now* and in the *future*. This can be accomplished by comparing the numbers in column 2 with those in column 3 and entering the differences in the appropriate spaces in column 4.

Step 6 • He should develop a realistic action plan for his growth and development as a manager. This will involve establishing objectives, identifying available resources and opportunities, and developing the plan itself.

MANAGER COMPENSATION

Though management has traditionally placed a great deal of importance on money as a motivational device, the problem of motivation is not so simply solved. An individual's needs are reflected in a very complicated pattern of latent and active motives. Money means different things to different people. Its relative value as a motivating force varies not only from person to person, but from situation to situation and from time to time. Nevertheless, a sound and equitable compensation system is a necessary condition for proper motivation and successful performance. Salary and wages are generally used to reward significant achievement, to encourage individuals to strive for advancement, to stimulate improved performance and results, to recognize status and achievement, to foster a sense of loyalty, and to attract and retain superior people.

Opsahl and Dunnette (1966) suggest that money plays both a "hygienic" and a "motivating" role in organizations. They take issue with the conclusions of Herzberg et al. (1959) that money acts only as a potential dissatisfier. More careful examination of Herzberg's data reveals that salary was mentioned as a major reason for unusually good job feelings 19 percent of the time. Of the unusually good job feelings that lasted several months, salary was reported as the reason 22 percent of the time; it was a causal factor of short-term feelings 5 percent of the time. In contrast, salary was named as a major cause of unusually bad job feelings only 13 percent of the time. It was mentioned only 18 percent of the time (in contrast with 22 percent) as the reason for unusually bad feelings.

McClelland (1972) suggests that the real value of money is "in the eye of the beholder." He views incentive plans as a means for managing motivation along the lines discussed in Chapter 6. Among other things, McClelland argues that whether an individual is high or low in the need for achievement (n–Ach) makes a real difference in the effectiveness of financial incentives. He cites research that indicates that additional financial rewards for doing a task do not make people with high n–Ach work harder or better. They do, however, influence people with low n–Ach. McClelland suggests that offering a bonus to salesmen with high n–Ach is not what produces the extra effort, although they would be angry if their extra effort were not recognized with a greater reward. On the other hand, it is not the task that interests people with low n–Ach. They will work harder for the increased financial rewards because the money has other values for them. Money was also found to be important for people with either high affiliation or high power needs. McClelland concludes that what will motivate a person with high or low need achievement will not necessarily motivate someone with a high need for power. Even though the cost of an incentive is identical, its form and meaning have to be shaped in a way which matches the needs of the people it is designed to influence.

According to Gellerman (1963), the most subtle and most important characteristics of money lie in its power as a symbol. In and of itself money has no intrinsic meaning. It is what money can buy, not the money itself, that gives it value. However, it also acquires motivating power when it symbolizes intangible goals. It acts as a symbol for different people in different ways, and for the same person at different times. Gellerman presents the idea that money can be used as a projective device; that is, that an individual's reaction to money is a summary of his biography. It reflects such things as his early economic environment, his competence training, his nonfinancial motives, and his current financial status.

The view that the value of money is symbolic, that it is indeed in the eye of the beholder, was dramatically illustrated by an energetic and highly successful young millionaire during a recent newspaper interview. When asked what drove him so hard and led him to take such great risks in business, he was quoted (by the *Los Angeles Times,* Sunday, February 25, 1973) as saying:

> The name of the game is money. I amass money because it measures the success of what I am doing, the way time measures a runner's speed. I am compelled to know how good I am.

Although there is an abundance of research literature on the subject of compensation, most of the studies deal with employee needs and preferences. Only a few deal with the preferences of managers for alternative forms of compensation. Mahoney (1964) reports one such study which has relevance for us here. The research involved a sample of 150 to 190 managers in each of three large corporations. A total of 459 managers, selected randomly from all levels in each organization, participated in the survey. Their preferences for the following general types of compensation were measured and analyzed:

1) Individual salary compensation.

2) Current individual incentive compensation, such as a bonus for achieving a given level of performance.

3) Deferred individual incentive compensation, where the bonus is paid to the individual at a later date (e.g., retirement or separation).

4) Current group incentive compensation, such as profit sharing, where the total fund is allocated annually and payments made to the individual as a portion of his salary.

5) Deferred group incentive compensation, derived from profit sharing as above, but where individual payments are withdrawn later upon retirement or separation.

6) Pensions, where the compensation takes the form of contributions to a pension fund.

7) Company-paid insurance, including life, medical, dental, and other plans.

8) Vacation, where the company pays for additional time off.

Other benefits, such as company-paid memberships and scholarships for children, were also included. Stock options, however, were excluded because of the difficulty of measuring their current value to the individual manager. Also omitted were expense accounts and nonmonetary forms of compensation such as tuition refunds and status symbols.

Participating managers were asked to indicate their preferred allocation of total compensation among the different forms. As indicated in Table 8–1, they preferred to have the largest portion of their com-

TABLE 8–1.   Manager Preferences for Salary as a Proportion of Total Compensation. Source: Mahoney, 1964. Reprinted by permission of Industrial Relations.

PERCENTAGE OF MANAGERS

DESIRED SALARY PERCENTAGE	COMPANY A (N = 147)	COMPANY B (N = 125)	COMPANY C (N = 124)
Above 95	1	18	17
85–95	17	28	27
75–85	66	32	33
65–75	13	18	8
Below 65	3	4	15
	100%	100%	100%

pensation in the form of salary. In company A, for example, 84 percent of the managers wanted their salary to be *at least* 75 percent of their total compensation. The response was only slightly different in the other companies. The preferred salaries as percentages of total compensation in the three companies were grouped around the following medians: 76 percent in company A, 82 percent in company B, and 83 percent in company C.

Managers were also asked to rank the various forms of compensation in order of their preference for each as a small increase in total compensation. As indicated in Table 8–2, salary was the most preferred form of increased compensation, while current incentives were generally preferred to deferred incentives. In two companies additional compensation in the form of vacation was least preferred by the managers.

Mahoney also analyzed the relationships between compensation preferences and the personal characteristics and circumstances of the manager. These included such things as age, number of dependents,

TABLE 8–2.   Manager Preferences for Form of Increase in Total
              Compensation. Source: Mahoney, 1964. Reprinted by
              permission of Industrial Relations.

MEDIAN PREFERENCE RANK

FORM OF COMPENSATION	COMPANY A	COMPANY B	COMPANY C
Salary	1	1	1
Current individual incentives	4	2	2
Current group incentives	2	3	3
Deferred individual incentives	7	4	6
Deferred group incentives	3	5	7
Pension	5	6	4
Insurance	5	7	5
Vacation	6	8	8

tenure, salary level, family income, net worth, and job type. Following
are some of the reported differences:

1) *Salary preferences.* Managers who preferred a relatively
large portion of their compensation in the form of salary tended
to receive below-average salaries and reported below-average
family income. They also tended to be younger and had less
tenure with the company. On the other hand, managers who
preferred a relatively small portion of their compensation in the
form of salary received above-average salaries, reported above-
average family income and net worth, were older than average,
and had above-average tenure with the company. Mahoney
concludes that variables such as age, tenure, salary, income, and
dependents tend to be interrelated and that these findings are
consistent with the belief that salary preferences are determined
by individual needs as well as by income tax considerations.

2) *Incentive preferences.* Managers who preferred current
incentives (individual or group) and individual incentives
(current or deferred) were younger than average. Conversely,
those managers who preferred deferred incentives and group
incentives tended to be older than average. It appears that
managers who are relatively more secure financially may tend

to gamble on incentives more than those who are less financially secure. And it also appears that younger managers prefer to gamble on their own personal performance, while those who are older have a desire to postpone the receipt of income.

3) *Pensions.* As one might expect, managers who preferred relatively high pension contributions were on the average older, reported above-average net worth, and had relatively longer tenure with the organization. Their children were also above-average in age.

4) *Vacations.* Managers who preferred increases in vacation time to other forms of compensation tended to earn below-average salaries and were from lower levels of management.

These and other findings generally support the popular notions held in many organizations. Mahoney (1964) reports, for example, that General Dynamics believes that younger managers with larger numbers of young dependents and relatively smaller incomes and net worth prefer more insurance and salary to other forms of compensation. On the other hand, older managers with fewer young dependents and with relatively larger incomes and net worth prefer various forms of deferred compensation. This is generally consistent with the notion that younger, less established, and less financially secure managers with large family responsibilities tend to prefer current payments. It should be recognized, however, that while preferences can be explained in terms of personal characteristics, the influence of a given characteristic is far from uniform. Mahoney notes that while managers who prefer larger salaries in proportion to their total compensation are younger than average, young managers as a group are no more inclined toward salary compensation than are older managers. Preferences are apt to be related more to a combination of circumstances than to any single characteristic.

There are thus several key questions which must be dealt with in manager compensation. These generally center around both the amount of compensation and the manner in which it is to be paid. The amount of compensation may consist of a *basic salary,* which includes fringe benefits and is generally related to the managerial job, and an *incentive or bonus,* which is generally related to the manager's contribution. A successful compensation program is one which considers and builds these elements in a way which best meets the specific needs and circumstances of the individual.

Basic salary

Salary and fringe benefits generally make up the largest element in most management compensation plans. Although an individual's basic salary depends upon his skill and ability, it is also dependent upon the relative worth of the position itself. Managerial jobs differ in terms of their difficulty, the amount of skill required, working conditions, the amount of responsibility they entail, and many other factors. Although a number of "job evaluation" techniques are available, the determination of a basic wage and salary structure for managers is at best an inexact science. A great deal of judgment is required. This is especially true at the higher levels of management. Regardless of the difficulty, however, every attempt should be made to develop a basic salary which reflects the relative worth of the job and is consistent with the needs of the individual manager.

Incentive compensation

An incentive or bonus plan can be an extremely important element in manager compensation. This is especially true when objective measures of performance are available. While the basic salary for a given position is generally tied to the relative worth of the job itself, incentive compensation may be tied directly to an individual's current performance. It reflects the actual contribution made by the individual in terms of organizational goals and objectives.

To be truly effective, however, the bonus should represent a reward for extra effort. It should neither be used to make up deficiencies in basic salary nor be awarded for performance and results which are merely acceptable. The award should be made only when and to the extent that the contribution is greater than the agreed-upon objectives or standards of performance. Effective incentive compensation provides for the following:

1) A clear understanding of the role of objectives and standards of performance in planning and measuring individual and group performance.

2) An appraisal system that guarantees that the rewards and incentives reflect recognition for performance which is *above* minimum standards.

3) A realistic cause-and-effect relationship between actual performance and the amount of the bonus.

4) Significant variations in bonus awards to reflect the realistic differences in performance and the actual contributions made by individual managers.

5) A common understanding of the role of the incentive plan and its relationship to the total compensation program.

While the above deals with the *amount* of salary and bonus paid to an individual, consideration also must be given to the *form* of compensation. As we have seen, the manner in which managers are paid can have a significant and direct impact on their level of motivation. Consequently, some deferred compensation plan should perhaps be an integral part of any effective compensation program for managers.

Most of the comments made about incentive plans can also be applied to deferred compensation plans. Stock options, for example, should be awarded in amounts that are consistent with base salaries, but their relationships to actual contributions and performance should be clear and direct. Too often their value as a motivating force is diluted because the purpose and meaning of the stock option plan is not clearly established and communicated to those concerned. It is important to highlight the requirement for *continued* contributions to organization growth and success.

As indicated in Figure 8–1, although current performance is an extremely important determinant of manager compensation, it is not the only consideration. Other factors may play a major role in determining the amount and form of compensation. Some are directly related to the individual himself, others are related to the organization, and still others are related to the external environment.

The individual • These factors generally include, among other things, the individual's actual current performance on the job; his performance relative to other managers; personal factors such as experience, education, and length of service; his present salary level; and the length of time since his last increase.

The organization • These factors include such things as the organization's ability to pay; the size of the merit pool or total amount of money to be distributed as increases; the salary treatment of other managers; the relative worth of the job itself; and the internal supply and demand for managers.

The environment • Among the considerations external to the organization are the general economic conditions; the external supply and demand for managers; industry compensation practices; and the availability of jobs in other companies.

In short, the compensation of managers is an important element in any system of management by objectives. An effective compensation program is one which provides a realistic basic salary according to the relative worth of the job and the individual needs of the manager. It also provides the basis for a cause-and-effect relationship between tangible rewards and good performance. Perhaps most important, however, it reinforces desired behavior and supports the other motivating factors in an MBO work environment.

CAREER AND MANPOWER PLANNING

As indicated in Figure 8–1, career and manpower planning is another important by-product of MBO and an integral part of the organization's long-range goals and strategic plans. The increased interest in management training and the rapid expansion of both external and in-house programs provide ample evidence of management's growing concern for identifying and developing future managers. Yet there continues to be an almost universal shortage of managerial talent. "Management obsolescence" is not just an academic buzz word. It is a fact of life in many organizations. Management itself is rapidly becoming a scarce resource. Why?

One explanation might be that the increasing size and complexity of modern organizations have accelerated the demand for managers. Another may be that nonprofit organizations are now in a better position to compete for and attract talented people. A better explanation, perhaps, is that most organizations fail to plan the use of their human resources in a systematic and imaginative way. Management training and manpower planning are directly related to the organization's strategic plans and the resulting changes in required management knowledge, skills, and qualifications. As one expert has written:

> By manpower planning I do not mean preparing replacement charts, listing jobs in the present organization that will become vacant in the next few years, or counting up the number of retirements and resignations to be expected each year. These are important and are legitimate parts of manpower planning, but manpower planning in its broadest sense is a

matter of anticipating the future pattern of organization, defining the skills and qualifications of managers at all levels in the future organization, deciding where managers with such skills are most likely to come from, and laying realistic plans for the necessary recruitment and development of such managers (Drucker, 1954).

Effective manpower planning, then, requires the following elements:

1) *Long-range goals and objectives.* To be effective, the manpower plan must be tied to the organization's goals and strategic plans for the future. These include well-expressed objectives in marketing, productivity, finance, physical facilities, and other key areas. Needless to say, the attainment of these objectives cannot occur unless there are enough competent people throughout the organization.

2) *A forecast of the future demand for managers.* Given the long-range goals and objectives, what is the likely demand for managers? How many managers will be required at the various levels to achieve the desired results? And equally as important, what kinds of qualifications will they need to be effective? An appraisal of the possible changes in management knowledge and skill profiles is essential to the forecast.

3) *An assessment of the current supply of managers.* This generally involves conducting an inventory of existing management resources. What is the age structure of our management team? When will various individuals retire? What turnover and attrition rates can we expect? Specifically, what knowledge, skills, and qualifications do the existing managers possess? What are their career interests and aspirations? This analysis may be made as required for each level or department. The assessment also involves an analysis of performance appraisal records to determine ratings in current performance and future potential.

4) *The identification and reconciliation of differences.* The identified gaps between current human resources and future requirements provide the basis for a comprehensive manpower plan. The plan itself represents an attempt to reconcile the differences between the supply and the demand for managers. It generally describes how they will be recruited, selected, promoted, and trained over a given period of time. It includes the

planned progression of managers from one job to another. As such, it also reflects career planning for the individual manager in that it helps him focus on the knowledge and skills required for his next job.

Manpower planning is a continuous activity. As such, it requires a certain amount of basic information which must be collected, updated, and kept current. Following are some illustrations of the nature and purpose of the data required to facilitate the process:

1) Updated vital information for all managers—to provide a basis for filling vacancies and to identify future training and development needs.

2) Regularly conducted *and* documented performance reviews—to provide a basis for compensation and to identify potential.

3) Assessments of the potential of each manager to assume more responsible positions—to provide a basis for filling vacancies and for developing individual career plans.

4) A classified listing of present management positions—to provide a basis for recruiting.

5) Job profiles and man specifications for each current position—to provide a basis for recruiting, selecting, and training.

6) A forecast of the number of managers required in the future for each classification—to provide a basis for recruiting and career planning.

7) A forecast of the job profiles and man specifications for future positions—to identify future training and development needs and to develop career plans.

8) Estimates of turnover and attrition rates—to provide a basis for recruiting.

The period of time covered by the manpower plan is generally determined by the time span of the organization's other strategic plans. Most writers are of the opinion that it takes from ten to fifteen years to develop a senior manager. Needless to say, it is virtually impossible to match supply and demand perfectly over a long period of time. Most organizations have either too many or not enough competent managers. If there is any danger in manpower planning, it is the danger of having too many competent managers. Most of us would agree that it is a danger worth risking.

REFERENCES

Drucker, P. F. *The Practice of Management.* Harper & Row, 1954.

Gellerman, S. A. *Motivation and Productivity.* American Management Association, 1963.

Herzberg, F., B. Mausner, and B. Snyderman. *The Motivation to Work.* Wiley, 1959.

House, R. J. *Management Development: Design, Implementation and Evaluation.* Bureau of Industrial Relations, University of Michigan, 1967.

Lippitt, G. L. *Organization Renewal.* Appleton-Century-Crofts, 1969, p. 210.

McClelland, D. C. "The role of money in managing motivation." In *Managerial Motivation and Compensation.* H. L. Tosi, R. J. House, and M. D. Dunnette, eds. Division of Research, Michigan State University, 1972, pp. 523–39.

Mahoney, T. A. "Compensation Preferences of Managers." *Industrial Relations* (No. 3, 1964): 135–44.

Opsahl, R. L., and M. D. Dunnette. "The role of financial compensation in industrial motivation." *Psychological Bulletin* 66 (1966): 94–118.

Installing the
MBO System

SOME PRACTICAL PROBLEMS

What is the best strategy for designing and installing the MBO system? Who should be responsible for its implementation? How long does it take? Who should participate in the process? And what kinds of problems can we expect and how can they be overcome? This chapter explores these questions in greater detail, from both theoretical and practical points of view, and provides some general guidelines for installing an MBO system.

Before we begin, however, it may be useful to discuss some of the practical problems encountered in attempts to implement a variety of MBO programs in a number of different organizations. Research seems to indicate that individual resistance to managing by objectives can take many forms: Managers may not understand it— "What is MBO?" They may not see the need for it—"I manage that way all the time anyhow." They may lack the skill—"My job doesn't lend itself to management by objectives." They may find it difficult to relate their jobs to organizational goals—"But I don't know what's really important." Or "My people always know what's expected of them," "I really don't have the time," "It's just another form to fill out," or "Yeah, but what's in it for me?" Most of these responses are symptomatic of the interrelated problems described below.

Lack of top management involvement and support

Several studies have stressed the importance of the top management commitment to managing by objectives. The active involvement and participation of upper levels of management is especially important to an MBO system which is tied to long-range organizational goals and strategic plans, as well as to overall performance objectives. Further, individual job objectives cannot be set in a vacuum. They require a backdrop of organizational goals and priorities, and, as we shall see later, top management involvement and support is generally required for any successful large-scale change effort.

Distortion in managerial philosophy

Several problems tend to emerge when managerial behavior is not consistent with the values and philosophy underlying MBO. Most systems are designed to increase management responsibility and participation at all levels of the organization. They are generally aimed at increasing *self*-motivation and *self*-control. Resistance to MBO tends to increase when the system is used as a "whip" or to increase "control" over subordinates. Such distortions tend to lead to numerical and statistical game-playing.

Difficulty of setting objectives

Some jobs and some areas of performance are difficult to measure and quantify. This is partly due to the nature of the job, partly due to the lack of data, and partly due to the lack of experience with goal setting. In some instances the problems can be dealt with by using "subjectives." In others, however, it may require training and experience.

Overemphasis on objectives

There is a human tendency to focus efforts only on those objectives which can be easily quantified and verified. Consequently, only a *part* of the total managerial job will be reflected in a set of objectives. This is especially true in the early stages of experience with MBO. Several studies have shown that an overemphasis on objectives can lead to short-run decision-making and neglect of other vital areas of performance. As we have seen earlier, maintenance objectives and standards of performance in these areas can help.

Increased paper work

There is also the danger of increasing the paper work burden on the already overloaded manager. This can easily happen if MBO is simply added to everything else he must do. A conscious effort must be made to ensure that data and reports that are no longer needed have been purged from the system. Perhaps most important, however, MBO must be properly integrated with other reporting systems.

Increased time pressures

Managing by objectives requires time for setting and reviewing objectives, for action planning, and for reviewing progress. Additional time pressures will be created if MBO is simply added to everything else that managers must do. The manager must learn to establish priorities and plan the use of his time more effectively. It helps when organizational goals and priorities are clearly communicated from above. It may also help to provide some managers with additional training in time management.

Lack of relevant skills

Contrary to what some of us would like to believe, the practice of MBO generally requires a set of skills and abilities which many managers do not have. They may need to develop skill in identifying and establishing key performance objectives—*and* the ability to express them in clear and concise terms; they may need to develop additional tools and techniques for action planning; and, most important, they may need to improve their interpersonal skills. MBO requires expertise in coaching, in counseling, in giving and receiving feedback, and in other areas of interpersonal communications. Manager training and organizational development are important considerations in the design and implementation of MBO systems.

Lack of individual motivation

As indicated above, the problem of motivation is complex. Individuals may not understand or see any need for MBO, or they may lack required skills or feel that top management is not really committed to MBO. Most important, perhaps, they may not see "what's in it for me." It helps to make the link between MBO and the reward and penalty system clear and distinct. It also helps to include personal development objectives as part of the individual's job objectives. And, as we shall see later, it helps when he is involved in the planning and implementation of the change to MBO.

Poor integration with other systems

If MBO is to be truly effective, it must be properly integrated with other management systems. This is no easy task. The goal-setting and review cycle must tie in to market forecasts, budgets, and other important processes and procedures. Careful planning and timing are required to help the transition to management by objectives and its integration with other systems. Depending upon the size and complexity of the organization, it generally takes time to "institutionalize" any major change in the organization's way of life.

Inappropriate change strategy

Implied in most of the above problems is the notion that MBO will fail, or will be less effective, if it is not properly implemented. Our experience indicates that this is so. Careful consideration must be given to such things as the way in which the system is designed, how it is to be introduced and installed, and who is to participate in the process if these problems are to be resolved. This generally requires that both the design and the implementation of an MBO system must be *planned*.

THE MANAGEMENT OF CHANGE

The introduction of a system of management by objectives generally requires significant changes in management philosophy and practice. Although the problems of organizational change are similar to the problems of change in individuals and small groups, they are considerably more complex. There are many more variables involved, the interactions are more numerous, and the consequences of the change are far less predictable. The impact on organization members, however, is generally the same. They face a new and different environment which makes new and different demands on them, and they are expected to respond appropriately to these new demands. That is, they must learn to behave in new and different ways. How can the undesirable consequences of these changes be minimized? How can we help to develop the kinds of behavior needed to be more effective in the new environment? Although the general subject matter is beyond the scope of this book, an attempt will be made here to deal with some of the issues involved in managing change. The focus will be on providing some conceptual tools and guidelines to facilitate the design and introduction of MBO in any given organization.

As most experienced managers well know, planning is essential to the effective management of change. This implies the existence of explicit change goals which are based upon a clear understanding of *what* is being changed, *why* it is being changed, and *how* it is to be changed. It is important at this point to recognize that the planning of change and its implementation are interdependent. The way in which a change is planned has an impact on the way in which it is carried out; conversely, the problems of implementing a change have an impact on the way in which it is planned. As we shall see, the planning of change is most effective when it is based upon a careful diagnosis of the environment.

The effective management of change also requires a systems approach to organizations and groups. One way of looking at a "socio-technical" system is to imagine that it consists of three major components or subsystems: the *technical* subsystem, including the technology involved, the flow of work, the required technical task roles, and a number of other technological variables; the *management* subsystem, including the formal organizational structure, policy, procedures, and rules, the ways in which decisions are made, and many other elements designed to facilitate the process of management; and the *social* subsystem, including essentially the organization's culture, its values and norms, the informal organization, the ways in which personal needs get satisfied, the attitudes of individual members, and numerous other personal, cultural, and human variables. The interactions *within* and *between* these subsystems produce the behavior and role relationships that affect organizational performance. Consequently, the effective implementation of change in any one of the subsystems also requires a careful consideration of its impact on the other subsystems of the organization. This generally involves the continuous, systematic collection and analysis of all of the relevant data.

Managers are sometimes misled by the apparent stability of the organizational setting. Actually, whenever people interact with each other over a period of time, the situation evolves into a state of "quasi-stationary equilibrium." The appearance of stability merely covers a constantly shifting set of forces. This view was first proposed by Kurt Lewin, a well-known social scientist and pioneer of social change (e.g., Lewin, 1947). Some of his basic concepts, graphically illustrated in Figure 9–1, still provide a useful way of thinking about the man-

FIGURE 9–1.   Quasi-Stationary Equilibrium. Source: K. Lewin, 1947. Adapted and reprinted by permission of Holt, Rinehart and Winston, Inc.

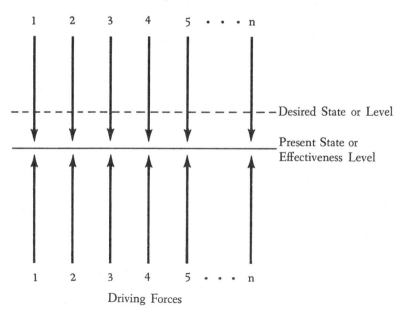

Driving Forces

agement of change. According to Lewin, any situation in which change is to be attempted may be viewed as a dynamic balance of forces working in opposite directions. One set of forces moves the situation in the direction of the anticipated change. These he calls the *driving forces.* The opposite set of forces, which tend to restrain or keep the situation from moving in the direction of the desired change, are called *restraining forces.*

The two sets of forces working against each other tend to create and maintain a state of dynamic equilibrium, a balance which can be disturbed at any point in time by altering either the driving or restraining forces which keep the situation in its present state or condition. A new level of equilibrium can be induced by increasing or adding to the driving forces, by decreasing or removing the restraining forces, or by some combination of the two. According to Lewin, however, an increase in the driving forces is apt to be accompanied by an increase in restraining forces, which results in an increase in tension or, at best, only a temporary change in the system. He concludes that *permanent* social change involves the following steps or phases:

> *"Unfreezing"*—by identifying and removing the forces opposing the change;
>
> *"Moving"*—by increasing or adding to the forces which will move the system to the desired state or changed condition;
>
> *"Freezing"*—by reinforcing the desired behavior and stabilizing the system at a new level of equilibrium.

Lewin's conceptual framework provides some basic analytical tools which can be used to facilitate the introduction of MBO in an organization. A "force-field analysis" can help the manager identify the relevant forces which might help or hinder the change effort. What are the forces which will tend to oppose the installation of MBO in my organization or department? How can they be minimized? What are the forces which will help to move us in the desired direction? How can I take advantage of them? How can we reinforce the desired behavior and keep from slipping back to our old ways of doing things? As the manager begins systematically to collect and analyze the data required to answer these questions, he becomes meaningfully engaged in the planning and implementation of an effective change program.

The first step in the implementation of change begins with an identification of the potential opposing forces. Resistive behavior is generally intended to protect an individual from the perceived effects of real or imagined consequences. The resistance may be expressed in a number of different ways, including apathy, hostility, aggression, low levels of aspiration, sloppy efforts, and poor performance. Following are only a few of the many common causes of resistance to change in organizations:

1) *There is a fear of the unknown.* People tend to feel secure when they know what to expect, how to respond, and what to do. They become anxious and uncertain when they are asked to exchange something that is familiar for something unknown.

2) *There is a need for security.* People also need a sense of predictability as to how things "fit together" in their world. They tend to resist changes which threaten to disrupt the stability of their environment.

3) *There are vested interests.* At times change may be perceived as a potential loss in personal status or power by those who are influenced by it.

4) *The nature of or reason for the change is not made clear.* People who do not understand the change or the reason for it tend to resist changes which affect them.

5) *There are different interpretations of the proposed change.* People tend to have different perceptions and views about change and how it is to be implemented. Information is easily distorted, especially in large organizations.

6) *The reasons for the change are not accepted.* Those affected by the change tend to resist when they do not feel the need for it. In this case, the degree of resistance is generally related to the amount of their participation in the process.

7) *There is a conflict of interests.* Because of their relationships outside of the situation, as well as their involvements in different groups, people tend to resist changes which conflict with their outside interests or group traditions.

8) *The change ignores the existing culture, values, or norms.* People also tend to resist change which is in conflict with the institutionalized patterns of behavior in the organization.

The process of *unfreezing* the system can actually begin with the collection of data required for a force-field analysis. Active and meaningful participation on the part of those affected can facilitate both the planning *and* the implementation of the change. The focus should be on those restraining forces which can have a significant impact on the change effort and about which something can be done. Once these are consciously selected and dealt with, the system can begin *moving* in the direction of the desired state or condition. This is generally accomplished by increasing one or more of the existing driving forces or by adding new ones to the field. The *freezing* or stabilizing of the system at a new level of equilibrium occurs as the new behavior is reinforced and becomes a way of organizational life. The management of change, then, is perhaps more of an art than it is a science. There are precious few guidelines to assist the manager, though in the search for usable criteria, a number of authors have attempted to identify some common patterns which have emerged from "successful" and "unsuccessful" change efforts. Larry Griener (1967), for example, has analyzed the published reports of some eighteen studies of planned change in organizations and found that several conditions required for success can be deduced from the list of characteristics he found common to the most successful change efforts:

1) The organization is generally under considerable external and internal pressure to improve. Top management has been aroused to action and is searching for solutions.

2) An intervention takes place at the top of the organization in the form of a catalyst who is either a new member of or a consultant to the top management team. This generally induces a reassessment of past practices and a reorientation toward current problems.

3) Top management assumes an active and direct role in the process. Several levels of management generally participate in the analysis and collection of relevant data.

4) New ideas and methods are generated at several levels in the organization. This generally results in some level of commitment to change by the organization's members.

5) Some degree of experimentation with innovation takes place. The proposed solutions are generally developed, tested, and found acceptable before the scope of the change is expanded to include larger problems or the entire system.

6) The program is generally reinforced by positive results. The change effort spreads with each success experience and, as management support continues to grow, is gradually accepted as a way of life.

Richard Beckhard (1969), on the other hand, has identified a number of conditions which seem to contribute to the failure of organizational change and development efforts:

1) The existence of a credibility gap between top management's statements of philosophy, values, and practices and their actual behavior.

2) The use of pieces of an MBO program or ad hoc activities which are not based on specific change goals.

3) A short time perspective or an unrealistic expectation of short-term results.

4) An over-dependence on and improper use of external and internal consultants.

5) A lack of communication and integration of MBO efforts between various levels within the organization.

6) The perception of "good relationships" as an end goal of MBO rather than as a *condition* for its success.

7) The search for quick solutions or cookbook prescriptions for organizational health and effectiveness.

8) The application of MBO in an inappropriate manner (i.e., without proper data gathering and diagnosis).

A more detailed description of how some of these concepts are applicable in the real world is provided in the two case studies which follow. As we shall see, there is more than one way to introduce and implement a system of management by objectives.

TRADITIONAL APPROACHES: A CASE STUDY

Traditional approaches to the introduction of MBO in large-scale organizations tend to begin with a policy statement or mandate from top management. The responsibility for the design and implementation of the program usually then falls to one of the staff or service groups, which conducts a pilot program to work out all of the details of the program, develops appropriate forms and procedures to facilitate its use, provides instruction manuals, and conducts extensive "orientation" or "training" sessions to ensure that the system is understood and properly utilized throughout the organization. Such was the case with the Purex Corporation.

The management philosophy at Purex was described by the president of the corporation in 1961 as ". . . a philosophy of management that stimulates the individual who has a desire to achieve, who possesses initiative, who is creative, and who is reaching for better things." [1] The policy statement, which established MBO as a vehicle for implementing this philosophy,[2] was issued in July of that same year and made several major points. First, the policy clearly established goal setting as an approach to management:

> It is the policy of the company to have every manager work with his immediate supervisor to set goals and objectives for his area of operation and to establish controls to assure their attainment [and, to the extent possible, to express these in measurable or tangible terms].

Second, the policy differentiated between financial and operational controls and the method of establishing them:

> Budgetary and other financial controls, financial information reporting, and all accounting procedures are established by the Vice-President of Finance.
> Operational controls (i.e., controls needed by Subsidiary or Division Heads, Department Directors, Regional Managers, Division Superintendents, Plant Managers, and all other supervisory personnel, for the proper evaluation of progress against forecasts and targets) will be established through the cooperative effort of the Management Analyses and Services Department and the operating manager concerned.

Third, the policy specified the manner in which goals and objectives were to be established:

> Subsidiary and Division Heads and all other supervisory personnel are responsible for setting verifiable objectives in their operating areas. These must be set for each operating period— e.g., a week, a month, a quarter, a year.
> Where assistance is needed in goal-setting, it is the responsi-

---

1. *From a speech given by Mr. Al Stoneman before the Research Committee of the Los Angeles Chamber of Commerce on April 25, 1961.*
2. *Company Policy # Management-5, dated July 31, 1961, effective August 7, 1961.*

bility of the manager's immediate supervisor to provide such assistance, and also to review and approve the goals and objectives.

Fourth, the policy specified who was to receive the control data:

> The purpose of establishing measurable controls is to supply information directly to the individual who is responsible for a definite area of operation so that he may on his own initiative act to correct any deficiencies and report the corrective action to his supervisor.

And finally, the policy provided for the periodic review and revision of goals as may be required:

> After goals, objectives, and targets have been established, it is the responsibility of Subsidiary and Division Heads to establish a schedule of periodic performance reviews and to recommend necessary changes in goals and objectives.

The responsibility for implementing the policy was assigned to the corporation's Management Analyses and Services Group (MASG). Top management also decided to "experiment" first with the new system in one of the older and more established divisions of the corporation. MASG spent the next three months conducting a pilot program in one of the largest plants in the division. During this time, the details of the goal-setting and review system were ironed out, including the identification of key result areas and the generation of the kinds of information needed to manage by objectives. MASG also developed appropriate instruction manuals, forms, and procedures required to implement the system throughout the division.

"Goals and Controls" was formally introduced as a viable MBO system in October 1961, some three months after the policy statement which gave it birth. MASG teams spent from two to four weeks at each plant to conduct on-site training and to facilitate the installation of the system. By January 1962, "Goals and Controls" had been introduced and was in operation in all of the fifteen plants of the division. It was next introduced in the marketing department and was in operation throughout most of the division a year later.

The company made its first real effort to assess the effectiveness of the program during the summer of 1963, some eighteen months after its introduction (for a detailed report of this study, see Raia, 1965). The findings were generally favorable. The productivity of the individual manufacturing plants had improved considerably. Before the introduction of "Goals and Controls," average productivity for all plants was decreasing at a rate of approximately 0.4 percent per month. During the first eighteen-month period, average productivity was 18 percent higher and increasing at a rate of approximately 0.3 percent per month. The increase in productivity was accompanied by improved morale and an increase in the level of motivation in most of the plants. It was also noted, however, that lower levels of management were not yet meaningfully participating in the process and that the program had imposed an additional administrative burden on the operating managers. An attempt was made to correct these deficiencies.

The findings of a second study a year later (Raia, 1966) generally supported those of the original. Productivity in all plants was still high. Success was generally attributed to the fact that MBO improved management planning and control on the job and provided motivation to improve individual job performance. It was noted, however, that productivity had leveled off to a rate increase of only 0.02 percent per month. It was also evident that the program was still not fully implemented at the lower levels, and that the administrative burden had not decreased. Several additional problems emerged. There appeared to be some distortion in the managerial philosophy underlying the program. More than a dozen managers reported that it was "used as a whip" and that it "treats people like statistics." An equal number reported that it had become a statistics game which was based upon "unrealistic standards" and "unrealistic or unchallenging goals." There was also evidence of an overemphasis on the attainment of production goals and targets. Some managers complained that this was generally done at the expense of other goals, particularly those related to quality. And finally, there was some evidence that the program failed to provide any tangible benefits for the individual manager. In the words of one of them: "What does it really mean to the individual when he successfully meets his goals? How does he personally benefit, other than by a feeling of accomplishment and inner satisfaction? What does it mean to the individual when he fails to meet certain goals?" The answer to these and a number of other questions raised by the two studies failed to materialize as "Goals and Controls" gradually lost its identity as a driving force in the organizational environment.

It might be useful at this point to examine the Purex case in the light of the characteristics or patterns of change outlined above. How does the attempt to implement "Goals and Controls" compare to other successful change efforts? How does it compare to those which were unsuccessful? Which characteristics facilitated the implementation of the program? Which ones hindered it? The comparisons may provide some additional insights into the management of change.

Some facilitating characteristics

Although there were no great internal or external pressures to change, there was a definite orientation toward growth. Top management was aroused to improve performance.

The intervention took place at the top of the organization. The president, who was the catalyst in this case, relied heavily on the technical expertise of an outside MBO consultant. Together they formulated the basic policy and plan to develop the management practices that were to implement the new philosophy.

Top management gave birth to and, initially at least, actively supported the program.

A considerable amount of experimentation was done at the pilot plant. The proposed program was developed, tested, and improved prior to its implementation in other plants.

The program initially met with considerable success. As positive results continued, the change effort spread throughout the division.

The company took a realistic view of the length of time required to implement the program. There was no unrealistic expectation of short-term results.

The communication and integration of the change effort between the various levels of management was generally well planned.

Good relationships were not seen as an end in themselves, but rather as a necessary condition for the successful implementation of the program.

The company was not searching for quick solutions or cookbook prescriptions to improved organizational health and effectiveness.

A considerable amount of data was collected about the technical aspects of MBO prior to the pilot study. Additional data gathering and diagnosis were done at the pilot plant to ensure that the design of the new system was consistent with the realities of the operating environment.

Some hindering characteristics

Although top management gave birth to and was interested in the program, it did not become actively involved in the process. There were no "Goals and Controls" for the top team.

There was a limited amount of participation in the development of the new ideas and methods among the various levels of management. The new system was developed primarily by the MASG group, which conducted a pilot program and "educated" operating line managers in how to implement it.

Although the program met with initial success, the second study indicated that the program had not yet become a way of life. It was evident that appropriate managerial behavior was not being reinforced in a way which would stabilize, or "freeze," the system at the desired level of performance.

A credibility gap began to emerge between the management philosophy and practice underlying the program and the actual behavior of some of the managers.

Although "Goals and Controls" provided an integrated approach to goal setting and periodic reviews, it was essentially a Phase 2 MBO program (see Chapter 2). Operating goals were not derived from a clearly-defined corporate strategy, nor was the program clearly and systematically tied to management training, compensation, and manpower planning.

As indicated earlier, external and internal consultants were used primarily as technical resources who designed the program and trained others to use it. The implementation of the program was the responsibility of internal consultants (the MASG teams) who functioned more as "technical experts" than as "change agents."

Although integration of the program and communications between the various levels of the organization were well planned, there was little follow-up to ensure that the program was being implemented at the lower levels of management.

Most of the data gathering and diagnosis focused on the technical aspects of designing an effective MBO program. Considerably less attention was given to the problems of implementation and change.

ORGANIC APPROACHES: A CASE STUDY

Organic approaches to the design and installation of an MBO system are generally based upon organizational problem-solving. The planning and implementation of the change effort become an integral part of the process of change in the organization. The emphasis is on collecting all of the relevant data in the force field, conducting systematic diagnoses, and carefully planning the interventions into the system. Organic approaches tend to reflect many of the characteristics generally associated with the more successful change efforts. Top management is actively and directly engaged in the process; there is a great deal of participation throughout the organization; innovations are encouraged from all levels; there is a willingness to experiment with new ideas and methods; a sense of flexibility and progress pervades the effort; free and open communications are encouraged; and an attempt is made to develop a climate of mutual trust and collaboration. Such was the case with PQR, a medium-sized school district in southern California (for a business example, see Lasagna, 1971).

The process began when the newly-appointed superintendent attended a management workshop during the spring of 1969 and decided that MBO might be a good vehicle for improving the administration of his school district. The district had recently lost a bond election and was faced with the need to make better use of its existing resources, for, like most other school systems in California, it was experiencing a great deal of internal and external pressure to improve. An external consultant was called in to assist in the design and installation of an appropriate MBO system. He functioned primarily as a flexible resource to the school district. Depending upon circumstances, his role varied somewhere between "MBO expert" and "change agent." The superintendent and several key administrators, including two school principals, participated in the initial planning of the change effort.

The first phase of the effort was aimed at developing an understanding of and some insights into the nature and process of managing by objectives, developing some of the required basic management skills, and beginning the process of data collection and self-diagnosis. After careful deliberation, the initial planning group decided to limit participation in the first phases to members of the district staff and the school administrators. Teachers, students, and the community at large were to become more actively involved by the end of the first year. The superintendent prepared a preliminary statement on "The Need for Management by Objectives" and distributed it widely throughout the district. Reactions to the document were generally favorable. After a series of discussions with the relevant parties, he then outlined the basic plan proposed by the initial planning group (see Figure 9-2).

As indicated in the memo, the first session focused on a discussion of how the system worked and how it might be applied in a school system. At the end of the presentation and discussion period, each participant was asked to give his idea of the potential personal,

FIGURE 9–2.   Courtesy of PQR Unified School District, Southern
California.

May 21, 1969

MEMO TO: All Administrators

FROM: (The Superintendent)

SUBJECT: Basic Plan for Management by Objectives

Based upon our recent discussions, the MBO planning group has put
together a preliminary plan to get us started. Please put the following
dates on your calendars:

1. Wednesday, May 28th, from 9:00 a.m. to 12:00 noon
2. Wednesday, June 11th, from 9:00 a.m. to 12:00 noon

(The consultant) will meet with us on May 28th to provide us
with a broad overview of the philosophy and practice of Management
by Objectives. The focus of this first session will be on developing
an understanding of MBO and how we might implement it in our
school district. The June 11th session will essentially deal with the
practical aspects of "HOW TO DO IT."

During the month of July we will begin to formulate and write specific
objectives for 1969-70 for the district and for each of the elementary,
intermediate, and high schools. (The consultant) will meet with
us, individually and in small groups, to help evaluate and refine our
work.

In August, we will select a small task group to work with (the
consultant) to develop a preliminary design for our MBO system
and to formulate a plan for its implementation in our district.

Throughout the rest of the year, (the consultant) will meet with us
from time to time to help us to refine the design and to deal with some
of the problems of implementation.

Attached is some reading material to help us prepare for the sessions.

school or departmental, and district advantages and disadvantages of the
MBO approach. Small groups were then formed and asked to develop
a group list which reflected the views of their individual members. The
total group then met to discuss the small group lists and strive for a
consensus. Following are the results of the exercise:

Potential personal advantages:
1) MBO could provide a system which invites greater in-

sight on the part of each administrator, as well as each employee, toward himself and others.

2) It could provide a basis for establishing priorities and long-range objectives.

3) It could promote a greater feeling of identification with the overall objectives of the district.

4) It could provide a system for ascertaining and fulfilling goals set by the administrator for himself.

5) It could provide a system for identifying individual talents and interests as well as inherent limitations.

Potential school or departmental advantages:

1) MBO could provide a system whereby roles and responsibilities of school staff members are defined more precisely.

2) It could encourage better and more effective communication.

3) It could provide a basis for more sophisticated assessment and evaluation of both program and personnel.

4) It could result in better articulation and better cooperation through emphasis on common goals and philosophy.

5) It could increase staff involvement and identification with school and district goals.

6) It could result in a more cohesive and unifying approach on the part of the entire staff.

7) It could encourage more effective utilization of individual staff members' talents and time.

Potential district advantages:

1) MBO could provide a system whereby roles and responsibilities of staff members are defined and understood more thoroughly.

2) It could serve as a unifying influence throughout the district and thus provide better articulation between schools and levels.

3) It could increase overall productivity through increased staff involvement and better identification with district goals.

4) It could serve as a basis for establishing district priorities and minimizing the less essential parts of the program.

5) It could encourage a better flow of communication, especially upward.

Potential personal disadvantages:

1) MBO could significantly increase the amount of paper work.

2) It could result in uneasiness or insecurity in some individuals because of the break with the traditional approach.

3) It could result in a need for additional in-service training to cope with orientation and other procedural matters inherent in the system.

Potential school or departmental disadvantages:

1) MBO could result in a definite conflict between the needs of people and the goals of the school or organization.

2) It could point up a deficiency in the skills needed for resolving staff conflicts stemming from the goal-setting process.

3) It could result in difficulty in achieving a consensus on certain topics.

4) It could result in a breakdown of the traditional approach to communication, especially horizontal communication.

5) It could result in eliminating or minimizing the sophistication that traditionally accompanies the recognition of competency.

Potential district disadvantages:

1) It could result in a decrease of productivity because of overinvolvement of the staff with semantics and the mechanics of the system itself.

2) It could result in the loss of some rapport with the community because of its orientation to traditional staff position roles.

3) It could result in some morale problems if contrary but necessary decisions are reached.

4) It could result in the need for additional personnel time and resources, especially during the early stages of implementation and while the relevancy of MBO to an educational system is being tested.

5) It could result in some serious consequences for the district if the "risk" it took in implementing the system did not prove fruitful.

Thus, with the identification of some of the driving and restraining forces in the field, the process of unfreezing the system had begun.

The second phase of the change effort continued through the summer months. With the help of the consultant, overall district goals were formulated and priorities for the coming year established. Specific objectives were also developed for the district staff and for each school for the 1969–1970 school year. The emphasis was on formulating well-stated objectives and action plans for each management position in the district. The MBO planning group also completed its assignment during this period. The results of their efforts included a schedule of progress reviews for the remainder of the school year, a plan to conduct two "sensing" sessions, one in December and the other in May, to evaluate the MBO program, and a preliminary plan to involve teacher, student, and community groups in establishing district goals and priorities for next year. The four-hour sensing session in May was devoted to a comprehensive assessment of the impact of MBO in the district. There was general consensus on the following points:

Positive experiences with MBO

1) MBO provides an effective means for mutual goal setting and involvement, which provides continuity and direction for the overall educational program.

2) It creates a positive pressure to get things done.

3) It provides a means by which an administrator can objectively evaluate his own performance and progress.

4) Establishing performance objectives in advance improves the whole tone of communication (and evaluation) between people (principal-teacher, assistant superintendent-principal, etc.).

5) MBO provides for more efficient scheduling and use of time.

6) It places responsibility and authority where the action is.

7) It makes provision for people to set goals, try, and succeed or fail without undue pressure.

8) It creates a positive pressure to anticipate needs and problems.

Negative experiences with MBO

1) MBO's effectiveness is hampered by the inevitable operational crises which divert the energies of people away from their objectives.

2) There is some lack of integration and consistency with respect to goals.

3) Under present financial conditions, justice cannot be done to the MBO philosophy because of time restraints imposed by limited staffing.

4) The system involves additional paper work and is time-consuming.

The emphasis in the next phase was on getting greater teacher and community involvement in the goal-setting process. A series of three evening meetings were scheduled for the month of June. In attendance at each meeting were approximately 95 representatives from the Board of Education, the Parent-Teacher-Student Association (PTSA), the Faculty Council, the Citizens Bond Committee, and other community groups. The first session was devoted to developing an understanding of MBO and how it was being used in the district, and reporting to the community-at-large on how the district had performed relative to its 1969–1970 objectives and plans. The representatives were asked to return the following week with a proposed list of district objectives for 1970–1971. The second session was devoted to synthesizing and integrating the various lists into a preliminary set of objectives and priorities for the coming year. During the following two weeks, the district staff and school administrators modified them, translated them into MBO language, and outlined preliminary action plans to achieve them. These were presented, discussed, and further refined during the third session with the same group of community representatives. The objective of this final session was to get additional clarity and community acceptance of the objectives and priorities for the district. The summer was spent developing derivative objectives and action plans for 1970–1971, for each school and for each administrator in the district.

The rest of the year was devoted to implementing the plans, reviewing progress, and taking necessary corrective action. Part of each monthly management meeting was used to deal with problems and to improve the implementation of MBO. The problem-solving focus and emphasis on improving the system was becoming a way of life in the district as evidenced by a memo from the superintendent early the following year (see Figure 9–3).

SUMMARY AND CONCLUSIONS

Attempts have been made to implement MBO, in one form or another, in a wide variety of organizations. The list is almost endless. Business firms, school systems, government agencies, and even religious

FIGURE 9-3.   Courtesy of PQR Unified School District, Southern California.

February 26, 1971

MEMO TO: Members of the MBO Planning Group

FROM: (The Superintendent)

SUBJECT: Management by Objectives

Please read the attached report which summarizes the current status of MBO in the district.

Now is the time when we should begin discussing our plans for late Spring and Summer, which will mark the end of our second year of managing by objectives.

Here is what we need to discuss at our meeting on Thursday evening March 4th, at 8:00 p.m., in the District Board Room.

1. How we broaden the basis of involvement to get inputs and feedback from staff (certified and classified), students, community, and Board of Education.
2. How we assess our progress on the 1970-71 district goals and objectives.
3. How we establish 1971-72 district goals and objectives.

In two years this district has carried MBO as far, and probably farther, than any school district in the U.S. However, much remains to be done, and, as Superintendent, I have a plea to make. Let us not dwell on what we have or have not done, but rather let us concern ourselves with what needs to be done next.

(The consultant) will be with us to "bring us up to speed" and to help us develop our future plans.

institutions, large and small, both here and abroad, have had some experience with something labeled "management by objectives." Some attempts have been successful and others have failed. What has been learned from these many attempts? The answer, of course, depends upon your frame of reference and experiences.

Ours might lead us to the following conclusions:

1) There is no one best design for a system of management by objectives. While the conceptual framework and guidelines contained in this and in other books provide good references, the system itself must be adapted to suit the given organization.

It must be designed in a way which is consistent with the realities of organizational life—technology, structure and processes, management philosophy and practices, and culture and norms, as well as the personal styles and preferences of the managers. The greater the differences, the greater will be the need for the effective planning and implementation of the change effort.

2) There is more than one way to install and implement an MBO system. The way in which it is introduced in an organization depends upon the nature of the technical task to be performed, the size of the organization, the geographic proximity of its subunits, the way in which major changes have been introduced in the past, and many other important considerations. Given what is presently known about the management of change, however, an organic approach to the design and implementation of MBO may be most effective. Organic approaches tend to be more responsive to changing requirements and ensure a better "fit" between the system and the organization.

3) MBO is both an instrument of change and a vehicle for dealing with the dynamics of change. It can be used to increase participation in organizational processes, improve management practices, change the organization's culture and values, and motivate its members. In this sense, it is itself an instrument for changing the organization. When it is used as a goal-setting, action planning, periodic review process, on the other hand, it becomes a vehicle which enables management to cope more effectively with the dynamics of a rapidly changing environment.

4) Management by objectives reflects a systems approach to management. It should not be viewed as *only* a philosophy, or a concept, or a performance appraisal technique, or a tool for more effective planning and control, or any one of its other aspects. It is both systemic and systematic. Whatever its initial form, it should eventually be tied to the organization's long-range goals and strategic plans and clearly linked to manager training, compensation, career and manpower planning, and other important activities and functions. MBO is most effective when it is properly integrated with key management processes and becomes a "way of managing" the organization's resources.

5) Top management is an extremely important reference group. Top managers must actively support and be directly involved in the MBO process. Individual job objectives become

more relevant when they can be tested in the light of higher-level goals and objectives. Goal setting is least effective, and can actually be frustrating, if it is done in a vacuum. Although it is not absolutely essential, MBO is most effective when it begins at the top and is gradually extended down through the organization.

6) The design and use of MBO should be based upon a sound diagnosis of the needs of the organization. This involves continuous collection and analysis of the data relevant to how the system is functioning and how it can be improved, as well as the data needed to formulate objectives and action plans. Effective implementation requires constant attention and monitoring of progress.

7) A different set of knowledge, skills, and attitudes is required to manage by objectives. Despite the insistence that "we do things this way all the time," MBO usually involves a change in managerial behavior. This suggests that "orientation" is not enough. Successful implementation generally requires management training and organizational development activities. Training is required to improve individual knowledge, attitudes, and skills. Organizational development is required to reinforce learning and to improve the way in which the key management processes are carried out. It might be well to remember that learning, or relearning, takes time and a considerable amount of effort, requires timely feedback, and involves a sense of progress on the part of those concerned.

8) MBO becomes an administrative burden when it is simply added to all the other things a manager must do. The pressures of time are more apt to be felt if it is something that must be done "in addition to" rather than "instead of." MBO is most effective when it is properly integrated with other management functions in a way which helps the manager do a better job.

9) And finally, the inclusion of personal objectives reinforces the MBO process. Personal growth and development objectives facilitate training and career planning. They provide an opportunity to integrate some individual needs with work-related activities. They also strengthen an individual's motivation and self-control. Perhaps most important, however, is the tangible stake they give him in the outcome. He is more apt to become meaningfully involved with and committed to the *total* set of objectives when he knows "what's in it for him."

In summary, then, introducing a substantially different management system in any organization can be a complex and time-consuming task. There is a considerable amount of evidence that management by objectives is an excellent way to manage human and nonhuman resources. Properly implemented, it can improve organizational effectiveness and health. But it is not a panacea. Neither its successes nor its failures can be attributed to any single element or thing. Like any other management system, it can be no more effective than the way it is used.

REFERENCES

Beckhard, R. *Organization Development: Strategies and Models.* Addison-Wesley, 1969, pp. 93–96.

Griener, L. "Patterns of organizational change." *Harvard Business Review* 45 (May–June 1967): 119–30.

Lasagna, J. B. "Make your MBO pragmatic." *Harvard Business Review* 49 (November–December 1971): 63–69.

Lewin, K. "Group decision and social change." In *Readings in Social Psychology.* T. H. Newcomb and E. L. Hartley, eds. Holt, Rinehart & Winston, 1947, pp. 340–44.

Raia, A. P. "Goal-setting and self-control." *Journal of Management Studies* 2 (February 1965): 34–53.

Raia, A. P. "A second look at management goals and controls." *California Management Review* 8 (Summer 1966): 49–58.

Annotated
Bibliography

SELECTED BOOKS AND MONOGRAPHS

Batten, J. D. *Beyond Management By Objectives.* American Management Association, 1966.

This is a description of managing by objectives which goes beyond the goal-setting step in the process. The establishment of objectives and targets, in and of itself, is not enough. Human resources must be properly integrated with money, facilities, materials, and other organization resources. A climate which facilitates individual motivation is required for improved performance and organizational effectiveness. The author suggests a seven-phase program designed to move MBO beyond the setting of goals. He also includes a number of illustrations and exhibits to facilitate its implementation.

Beck, A. C., and E. D. Hillman. *A Practical Approach to Organization Development through MBO: Selected Readings.* Addison-Wesley, 1972.

The focus of this book is on the use of MBO as a vehicle for organizational development (OD). Selected readings are used to cover

173

many of the vital areas of both MBO and OD. They are well selected and include the works of many well-known writers in the field. Overall, the book provides the practicing manager with a broader view of the dynamic environment of his organization and the factors involved in implementing an MBO system.

Carroll, S. J., Jr., and H. L. Tosi, Jr. *Management By Objectives: Applications and Research.* Macmillan, 1973.

Written for both the student and the practitioner, this book reports on the existing research findings relative to MBO and develops some practical guidelines for designing and implementing an MBO program. The authors conclude that this approach can improve organizational planning and managerial performance and attitudes. They caution, however, that MBO will fail or not live up to expectations if it is not given adequate support and is not well integrated into the organization. Numerous suggestions and operating guides are provided throughout the book. These generally focus on the implementation of MBO, on goal setting, on carrying out the review process, and on integrating MBO with other systems.

Drucker, Peter F. *The Practice of Management.* Harper & Row, 1954.

This book contains what is perhaps the first definitive statement of the theory and practice of management by objectives. Although much of the volume is essentially a general description of the role of management in organizations, the author devotes several chapters to the MBO philosophy and process. The job of management, according to Drucker, is to balance a variety of needs and goals "in every area where performance and results directly and vitally affect the survival and prosperity of the business." He further defines these areas to include (1) market standing, (2) innovation, (3) productivity, (4) physical and financial resources, (5) profitability, (6) manager performance and development, (7) worker performance and attitude, and (8) public responsibility. Drucker also provides a brief description of how and by whom objectives should be set.

Enell, J. W., and G. H. Haas. *Setting Standards for Executive Performance.* American Management Association Research Study #42, 1960.

This is the first of a series of AMA monographs which deal

with results-oriented performance appraisal. In addition to defining standards of performance and describing how they can be set for executive jobs, the authors report on several case studies. Developing standards for executive performance, according to the authors, is generally based upon (1) breaking the job down into its major segments or tasks and (2) setting up standards which state *how well* each major task is to be accomplished. The authors also provide a number of useful guidelines for establishing standards and setting them down in writing.

Hughes, Charles L. *Goal-Setting: Key to Individual and Organizational Effectiveness.* American Management Association, 1965.

This is essentially a description of MBO which emphasizes the need for setting both organizational and personal goals in the process. Effective performance depends not only upon the validity of the goals, but on the degree to which company and individual goals can be integrated. The author explains in some detail the relationship between motivation and management. The emphasis is on how to recognize the human needs for self-fulfillment and job satisfaction and stimulate goal-setting behavior. He also describes how overall objectives can be broken down into subgoals at all levels of the organization.

Humble, J. W. *Improving Business Results.* McGraw-Hill, 1968.

Improving business results requires setting company objectives and improving the performance of management. The author defines MBO as a "dynamic system which seeks to integrate the company's need to clarify and achieve its profit and growth goals with the manager's need to contribute and develop himself." His emphasis is on the improvement of performance through the clarification of organizational objectives and the development of individual job improvement and training plans. A typical sequence for introducing the program, some common problems in organization and control, and the implications for top management are discussed in some detail. The author also describes the experience of three foreign companies who have installed the program.

Humble, J. W. *Management By Objectives in Action.* McGraw-Hill, 1970.

This is a good supplement to the author's earlier text which shows, primarily with case material written by the people closely involved, how the system works. The author himself describes some of the basic concepts of MBO and provides editorial comments on the selected readings. The case studies describe the experiences of a variety of British organizations and reflect a common pattern of conditions for success. These include committed leadership from the top, flexibility in method and technique, the use of high quality MBO advisors (consultants) at the launching stage, and constant attention and leadership to ensure that the momentum is maintained. A number of the readings highlight some of the problem areas and special difficulties met in applying MBO and show how they can be overcome. The author concludes with an "action programme" consisting of a series of questions and check lists designed to stimulate the reader to put the system in his own organization.

McConkey, D. D. *How to Manage By Results*. American Management Association, 1965.

This is essentially a pragmatic approach to MBO as a vehicle for planning and evaluating managerial activities in terms of results. The process generally begins at the top (but does not have to) with the establishment of broad overall corporate objectives as the basis for tactical objectives, strategic objectives, and short-term targets. Results-oriented objectives are thus set for each successive level of management. Throughout the book, the author provides some useful guidelines for installing and administering an effective MBO program. One chapter is devoted solely to asking and answering a number of key questions. The author also provides a brief description of some successful case studies.

Mali, Paul. *Managing By Objectives: An Operating Guide to Faster and More Profitable Results*. Wiley, 1972.

The total mission of an organization, according to this author, is accomplished by breaking it up into several phases, developing operating plans for each phase, involving managers in their implementation, and setting a time scale for the completion of each phase. MBO is described as a five-phase process: (1) finding the objective; (2) setting the objective; (3) validating the objective; (4) implementing the objective; and (5) controlling and reporting status of the objective. A number of unique concepts, guidelines, and illustrations designed to facilitate each phase in the process are provided throughout the book.

Miller, Ernest C. *Objectives and Standards: An Approach to Planning and Control*. American Management Association Research Study #74, 1966.

This is essentially an update of the earlier AMA report by Enell and Haas and is based upon information on the use of objectives and standards of performance in more than 100 companies. Nearly all companies using the MBO approach report important gains in executive concentration on vital company targets. Other findings include increased motivation, improved communication of important job-related information, and a better basis for compensation and training of managers. According to the author, most respondents believed that the use of objectives and standards is a fundamental aspect of managing and the very essence of the planning and control process.

Miller, Ernest C. *Objectives and Standards of Performance in Production Management.* American Management Association Research Study #84, 1967.

This is a continuation of the author's long-term study of the use of objectives and standards of performance in industry. In this report a distinction is made between objectives and standards. The emphasis of objectives, according to the author, is on those aspects of the managerial job that are to be improved. The focus is on change, on improvement, on implementing plans, and on ensuring that each job contributes to overall objectives. Standards of performance, on the other hand, are developed with regard to *all* of the elements of *one* managerial job and usually cover those areas for which there is little present economic justification for striving for improvement. This report also contains a brief description of the Rockwell Manufacturing Company approach and a more detailed description of General Electric's Goal-setting, Work Planning, and Review program.

Miller, Ernest C. *Objectives and Standards of Performance in Marketing Management.* American Management Association Research Study #85, 1967.

The emphasis of this report is on the importance of individual participation in the development of a hierarchy of objectives and performance standards for the marketing function. Although motivation is important throughout the organization, according to the author, it is especially important in marketing management. A brief description of the process of establishing objectives and standards and their relationship to budgets, performance appraisal, salary administration, and other aspects of management is provided. The author also provides a more detailed description of the application of objectives and standards in the marketing function of Univis, Inc.

Miller, Ernest C. *Objectives and Standards of Performance in Financial Management.* American Management Association Research Study #87, 1968.

This report deals with the use of objectives and standards in financial management. The emphasis is on developing measures that can be used to facilitate "management by exception." What is needed, according to the author, is an information system which provides a description of the results being attained and standards of performance against which the descriptions can be routinely compared so that deviations are immediately obvious. The author concludes that "attitude" is perhaps the most important aspect of MBO. He describes it as "aggressive commitment to ends which are consistent with the objectives and the needs of the organization and which are understood by managers, in each function and at each organizational level."

Morrisey, George L. *Management By Objectives and Results.* Addison-Wesley, 1970.

This is an elementary book on managing by objectives and results, labelled MOR by the author. This approach, in essence, breaks down the managerial job into its basic functions, selects those that are most important to the individual manager, and lays them out in an orderly and logical sequence of activities. Particular attention is paid to the costs associated with a given effort. Although the MOR process is described around the five basic management functions, the focus is on planning and controlling. Special emphasis is placed on defining roles and missions, forecasting, programming, scheduling, and budgeting as integral elements in the process. The author provides numerous illustrations and "how-to-do-it" examples throughout the text.

Odiorne, George S. *Management By Objectives.* Pittman, 1965.

This is an introduction to the philosophy, method, and process of managing by objectives. The general approach is to treat MBO as a system. In addition to providing a description of the process and some guidelines for setting individual and organizational goals, the author devotes several chapters to key questions and areas. These include the level and extent of subordinate participation in goal-setting, the relationship of MBO to salary administration, and the problem of the annual performance review. He also provides some guidelines to facilitate the implementation of MBO in an ongoing organization.

Odiorne, George S. *Management Decisions By Objectives*. Prentice-Hall, 1969.

This is essentially an expansion of the author's earlier book on MBO. The description is generally around setting objectives, gathering facts, identifying and specifying problems, searching for optimal solutions, taking action, and controlling the effects of decisions. The author also deals with some of the other aspects of managerial decision-making and practices. Included are the management of time, the art of managing, making snap judgments, and other considerations. The discussion of some of the tools for making decisions includes sampling and aspects of probability.

Reddin, W. J. *Effective Management By Objectives*. McGraw-Hill, 1971.

The focus of this book is on the concept of "effectiveness areas" and team implementation in MBO. Effectiveness areas, as defined by the author, reflect the "general output requirements of a managerial position." This is somewhat different from the notion of "key result areas" which stresses greater selectivity of job outputs. The author also believes that many firms try to achieve too much too soon and, as a result, tend to freeze the organization so that it is less able to cope with the changes required to implement MBO. "Unfreezing" is accomplished by a series of management team meetings (starting at the top) designed to ensure that managers understand the nature of MBO, and are capable of identifying effectiveness areas and of setting improvement objectives.

Schleh, Edward C. *Management By Results*. McGraw-Hill, 1961.

This approach to MBO is based upon the belief that better performance is directly related to the extent to which objectives are stated in terms of final measurable results. According to the author, individuals may easily lose sight of the central purpose of the enterprise if only the activities which are required of them are specified. Management objectives must be expressed in terms of the specific accomplishments expected from each individual. Goal-setting is essentially the job of the superior and is "the final expression of his delegation." The superior, however, consults with each subordinate before establishing the results expected of him. The author also advocates self-control as an integral part of results-oriented management.

Wikstrom, Walter S. *Managing By and With Objectives.* Studies in Personnel Policy, No. 212, National Industrial Conference Board, 1968.

This report deals briefly with the concept of MBO and more extensively with its implementation in five well-known companies who use MBO as a general approach to managing, rather than for some other more limited purpose. The author describes the procedures used to determine objectives, the degree to which they are quantified, and the mechanisms used to ensure that specific individual objectives do not conflict with those of others. He also examines the use of objectives in controlling operations and in appraising managerial performance.

SELECTED ARTICLES

Brady, Rodney H. "MBO Goes to Work in the Public Sector." *Harvard Business Review* 42 (March-April 1973): 65–74.

This is a description of the application of MBO in the Department of Health, Education, and Welfare. The author first discusses some of the problems that must be overcome before MBO can become effective in public-sector organizations. He then describes how it was made operational at HEW. A number of lessons that should prove to be helpful to both public- and private-sector organizations wishing to implement MBO are also drawn from the HEW experience.

Carroll, Stephen J., and Henry L. Tosi. "Goal Characteristics and Personality Factors in a Management By Objectives Program." *Administrative Science Quarterly* 15 (September 1970): 295–305.

This is a report of an MBO program in a medium-sized firm. The authors correlate different goal characteristics to the success of the program. Manager personalities and job factors were held constant. The results indicate that clear and important goals produce favorable results, especially for certain personality types. Difficult goals, on the other hand, increase the efforts of some managers and decrease the efforts of others. Although setting a large number of goals did not produce negative results, establishing priorities for the goals produced more positive feelings about the program. The degree of subordinate influence in the goal-setting process was not found to be related to goal-attainment, level of effort, or attitude toward the program.

Corey, Milton O. "Management By Objectives." *Training and Development Journal* 21 (September 1967): 57–63.

This is a description of the four phases involved in launching MBO at the John Hancock Mutual Life Insurance Company: *Phase 1*— goals and objectives for 1980 were established and communicated to all management and supervisory personnel during a management forum; *Phase 2*—each department was asked to prepare five-year and one-year plans to achieve the 1980 company goals; *Phase 3*—each person, from first-line supervisors up to department heads, prepared individual one-year job objectives; and *Phase 4*—together with their immediate management, employees selected areas of activity for which goals were to be set. The author also describes some of the problems and benefits experienced by the company.

Dove, Grant A. "Objectives, Strategies, and Tactics in a System." *The Conference Board Record* 7 (August 1970): 52–55.

The author, who is Vice-President of Corporate Development at Texas Instruments, Inc., describes the "Objectives, Strategies, and Tactics" (OST) approach to MBO used by the company. Emphasis is placed on strategic and tactical planning, as well as on the establishment of objectives. The system is also used for managing change and for developing managers.

Eastman, N. "MBO in R&D." *Business Management* (February 1970): 28–31.

This article describes how a management development program was integrated into the MBO system of an R&D department. The author provides sample forms and an example of a "Staff and Management Development Scheme."

Froissart, Daniel. "The Day Our President and MBO Collided." *European Business* (Autumn 1971): 70–78.

MBO will fail, according to this author, if its participative philosophy runs counter to an already existing authoritarian pattern of management. The effort will also fail if there is a lack of corporate objectives, if personnel welfare is neglected, or if the managers do not act as professionals. Successful MBO requires training of managers and the will of the president to make it work.

Glasner, Daniel M. "Patterns of Management By Results." *Business Horizons* (February 1969): 37–40.

This author points to the "semantic jungle" which exists in results-oriented management. He identifies five distinct patterns. These include Task Management, Job Management, Man/Job Management, Goal-Oriented Management, and Accountability Management. A matrix is used to summarize the elements and patterns of the various approaches.

Granger, Charles H. "The Hierarchy of Objectives." *Harvard Business Review* 42 (May-June 1964): 63–74.

The role and importance of clearly defined *and* balanced objectives are stressed in this article. There are goals within goals within goals, according to the author, and they all require painstaking definition and close analysis if they are to be individually useful and/or profitable as a whole. In addition to stating some criteria for testing the validity of an objective, the author describes the steps involved in the reiterative process of developing a clear and integrated hierarchy of goals. He also describes its practical uses and the tangible results that enhance organizational effectiveness.

Granger, Charles H. "How to Set Company Objectives." *Management Review* 59 (July 1970): 2–8.

In this article the author provides a list of eight criteria which can be used to test the effectiveness of objectives and describes how they can be formulated. The process involves first an analysis of relevant trends in the business environment and then the development of a comprehensive set of objectives in three areas: (1) financial; (2) product-market mix; and (3) functional areas such as technical, marketing, operations, and personnel. This provides for specific plans and action programs and a basis for developing objectives for individual managers which are tied to overall objectives and business plans.

Hill, Walter. "The Goal Formation Process in Complex Organizations." *Journal of Management Studies* 6 (May 1969): 237–48.

This is a somewhat general discussion of the way in which goals become established in formal organizations. The author suggests that organizational objectives are influenced by the external and internal tunity to learn. It has an essentially *cognitive* base and relies primarily on instruction and demonstration. The latter generally has an *experiential* base and occurs when the learning is internalized through practice and experience. Together, they provide the basis for individual learning and growth.

Because of the growing awareness of learning as both an internal and a continuous process, the training and development of managers is no longer an ancillary activity in most organizations. Indeed, there have recently been noted trends toward improved performance rather than increased individual knowledge; toward dealing with situations rather than individuals; toward seeing training as a management tool rather than as a departmental function; toward decreasing reliance on outside experts; and toward objective evaluation, feedback coordination, reinforcement, self-motivation, goal orientation, and homogeneity (Lippitt, 1969) in current thought about ways to develop human resources in organizations. The emphasis tends to be on improved performance, on the integration of "training" as part of the managerial job, on learning goals and on result-oriented education, on self-motivation, on the continuous nature of training and development, and on organizational climate as a factor in learning and change. Perhaps most important, however, is the recognition that the ultimate responsibility for learning rests with the individual.

Most of these trends are consistent with the underlying philosophy and system of management by objectives. House, for example, defines management development as

> . . . Any attempt to improve current and future managerial performances by imparting information, conditioning attitudes or increasing skills. Hence, management development includes such efforts as on-the-job coaching, counseling, classroom training, job rotation, selected readings, planned experience, and assignment to understudy positions (House, 1967).

MBO can facilitate both on-the-job and off-the-job training and development. It is in itself developmental in that it involves appraisal, feedback, counseling, and coaching. Although it generally occurs within the context of the work environment, it can also support and reinforce off-the-job training programs and techniques.

The importance of and need for self-development in MBO is based upon what we currently know about how people learn. To begin with, we know that learning is an *internal* process. It generally occurs when the individual experiences a problem or recognizes that there is a difference between where he is and where he wants to be. As such, it is essentially a problem-solving activity based upon self-inquiry. The individual then draws upon a teacher, a book, the experience of others, his own experience, or other available resources to acquire what he needs to know before he can act to solve the problem. The idea that he learns best from the conventional classroom situation is not consistent with modern psychological research. The teacher is only one of many resources, and the classroom is only one of many situations which facilitate the learning process. This suggests that managers can develop themselves if they know how to make use of all the resources available to them. It also suggests that there is no one best way to learn.

We know that learning is most effective when its purpose is *known* and *accepted* by the individual. This suggests that the existence of goals facilitates the learning process. If the individual knows what the expected outcomes are, he is more apt to become meaningfully involved. It also suggests that the learning goals must be relevant to and consistent with his own needs. These two conditions are most likely to occur when they are *his* goals and not those provided for him by someone else. One of the first steps required for self-development, then, involves diagnosing one's needs and translating them into realistic goals and objectives.

We also know that learning is an *active* process which involves a *change in behavior*. The individual learns best when he actively absorbs new values or knowledge and translates them into new behavior. He does not passively sit by while new ideas are stuffed into his head. And since there is a human tendency to resist change, he must actively seek ways to translate the new learning into action. This suggests that self-development is facilitated when the individual recognizes the need for and wants to change, when he becomes actively involved in acquiring new learning, and when he honestly deals with his own reluctance to modify his behavior.

Finally, we know that learning is enhanced by *feedback* and a sense of *progress*. Since management does not occur in a vacuum, the self-developing manager needs help from others. He needs to know the impact of his new behavior on his performance. He also needs honest reactions from those with whom he works—his boss, his subordinates, and his peers. He needs this feedback so that he can measure his progress and modify his goals. If he can see some evidence of improvement, or at least has some sense of progress, he is more apt to invest additional time and energy in the learning process. The self-developing manager, therefore, needs to see that the newly learned behavior is actually producing the desired results.

environment, by the internal power structure, and by the process of bargaining among individuals and groups. He also discusses the goal formation process in some detail.

Howell, Robert A. "A Fresh Look at MBO." *Business Horizons* (Fall 1967): 51–58.

This is an attempt to distinguish between MBO as an aid to appraising performance and as an approach to top management planning and control. According to the author, the primary thrust for MBO has come from behavioral scientists and personnel managers who see it as a way of increasing individual motivation and as a basis for evaluating job performance. Many advantages will be missed unless a broader view of MBO is taken. Top management must get actively involved in the process by establishing overall organizational goals and disseminating them throughout the organization. Individual objectives are then modified and communicated upward through the various subunits. The author suggests the use of peer groups at each level to facilitate lateral trade-offs and to ensure the horizontal consistency of goals. Top management must then integrate them and direct carrying them out.

Howell, Robert A. "Managing by Objectives—A Three Stage System." *Business Horizons* (February 1970): 41–48.

In this article the author modifies his earlier view that there are two dichotomous approaches to MBO. He now sees the development of an effective MBO system as a "normal evolution" involving three stages: (1) the performance appraisal stage; (2) the integration of objectives stage; and (3) the long-range planning stage. Although possibilities exist for reducing the average length of time required to pass through each of these evolutionary stages, the author sees no way for a company to shorten the time required for the sequence. It still takes four to five years to develop a fully effective MBO system.

Humble, John W. "Avoiding the Pitfalls of the MBO Trap." *European Business* (Autumn 1970): 13–20.

This is a good description of some of the problems encountered by the incomplete or faulty application of MBO in an organization. Avoiding the pitfalls, according to Humble, demands constant watching of the way the system is functioning. Are there good communications between lower and upper levels of management? Is the system being kept flexible? Are the objectives of *both* the company *and* its managers being taken into account? The technical and human aspects of the system are closely related. Concentrating on performance goals and neglecting the individual's development and fulfillment is the surest way to fall headlong into the pit.

Huse, Edgar E. "Putting in a Management Development Program That Works." *California Management Review* 9 (Winter 1966): 73–80.

    This is essentially a description of a pilot program involving the implementation of a Work Planning and Review (WP&R) program in one of the subunits of a large organization. WP&R was designed to replace a classic performance appraisal system which was not effective in improving work performance. After an initial failure, the program ultimately became successful. Results indicated that there had been a significant increase (72%) in specific actions taken to improve performance. Other non-research data pointed to similar positive findings. The author concludes that WP&R is effective as a management development program at all levels of the organization in a wide variety of management positions.

Ivancevich, John M. "The Theory and Practice of Management By Objectives." *Michigan Business Review* 21 (March 1969): 13–16.

    The MBO programs of two different organizations were studied and compared by the author. In one company, where the Personnel Director was the primary force in the implementation of MBO, there was little change in the need satisfaction of participating managers. In the other company, where top-level executives initiated the program and were very active in its implementation, the author noted considerable improvements in various need categories. He also summarizes a number of other findings and makes some tentative recommendations.

Ivancevich, John M., James H. Donnelly, and Herbert L. Lyon. "A Study of the Impact of Management By Objectives on Perceived Need Satisfaction." *Personnel Psychology* 23 (Summer 1970): 139–51.

    This is a more technical treatment of the above study. Their findings indicate that MBO is more effective when top-level executives explain, coordinate, and guide the program. This provides for a better understanding of the philosophy and mechanics of the program throughout the entire organization and a greater satisfaction of needs among lower level managers. In addition, it was found that the frequency of the goal-setting and feedback sessions also has some impact on need satisfaction. The authors stress the importance of top management involvement in the process, an appropriate amount of time devoted to feedback sessions, and the need for constant review to determine the ongoing effects of the program.

Ivancevich, John M. "A Longitudinal Assessment of Management By Objectives." *Administrative Science Quarterly* 17 (March 1972): 126-38.

The study of the implementation of MBO in two different organizations is continued in this report. In one of the companies, the impetus was provided through the personnel department; in the other, it was provided by top management. The author observes that managers in neither firm showed any significant improvement in need satisfaction thirty months after implementation and that the failure to reinforce what was learned through training might have been frustrating for participants and may have been the cause of the lack of improvement.

Kindall, Alva F., and James Gatza. "Positive Program for Performance Appraisal." *Harvard Business Review* 41 (November-December 1963): 153-66.

The shortcomings of "typical" performance appraisal systems are discussed by the authors, who favor a results-oriented approach. They provide a detailed description of a participative, five-step program which involves the following steps: (1) The individual discusses his job with his superior and they agree on the content and relative importance of his major duties; (2) the individual establishes performance targets for each of his responsibilities for the forthcoming period; (3) he meets with his superior to discuss his targets; (4) checkpoints are established and ways of measuring progress are selected; and (5) they meet again at the end of the period to discuss the results of the subordinate's efforts to meet the targets. The authors also provide some suggestions and guidelines for making the transition to this kind of performance appraisal program.

Kleber, Thomas P. "The Six Hardest Areas to Manage By Objectives." *Personnel Journal* 51 (August 1972): 571-75.

Although results-oriented MBO is a natural for managing production line departments, according to this author, it is difficult to implement in the following areas: (1) public relations; (2) engineering and research; (3) the controller function; (4) educational institutions; (5) nonprofit (voluntary) organizations; and (6) government agencies. He explains why each represents a "challenge" and suggests how MBO might be approached in each area.

Koontz, Harold. "Shortcomings and Pitfalls in Managing by Objectives." *Management By Objectives* 1 (January 1972): 6–12.

Most organizations are not realizing the full potential of their MBO programs, according to this author, because they are unaware of some of the problems that can be encountered. He identifies a number of pitfalls, many of which are in the areas of goal-setting and performance appraisal. He also provides some suggestions of how to avoid them.

Lasagna, John B. "Make Your MBO Pragmatic." *Harvard Business Review* 40 (November-December 1971): 64–69.

This is a description of an "organic" approach to the implementation of MBO. Too often management systems become ends in themselves, according to the author, rather than tools to help managers be more effective. This is especially true in large organizations. Formal MBO program approaches often alienate managers when they attempt to impose uniform procedures on a company-wide basis and when they attempt to cover too many management functions and activities. The author describes how the Wells Fargo Bank approaches these problems with an MBO process which is limited only to planning and control activities, and which is flexibly designed around the specific needs of small organizational groups. The implementation process is facilitated by internal consultants who serve primarily as change agents.

Leathers, James O. "Applying Management By Objectives to the Sales Force." *Personnel* 44 (September-October 1967): 45–50.

This is a description of the application of MBO in the Sales Department of the Emko Company. Flexibility was stressed in the implementation process, which included a review of the marketing plan, the indoctrination of field personnel to overcome the problem of geographical separation, and an experiment with field supervisors to work the bugs out of the program.

Levinson, Harry. "Management By Whose Objectives." *Harvard Business Review* 48 (July-August 1970): 125–34.

According to this author, MBO is "one of the greatest managerial illusions." The MBO performance appraisal processes, as typically practiced, are inherently self-defeating over the long run because they are based on a reward-punishment psychology that simply serves to increase pressure on the individual while giving him a limited choice of objectives. Although he does not reject the MBO process itself, the author argues that it can be improved by examining the underlying assumptions about motivation, by extending them to include group goal-setting and appraisal, by the appraisal of superiors by subordinates, and by considering the personal goals of the individual first.

McConkey, D. D. "Judging Managerial Performance: Single vs. Multiple Levels of Accountability." *Business Horizons* (Fall 1964): 47–54.

Measuring performance is very difficult under traditional performance appraisal and merit rating systems. An effective alternative, according to the author, is an MBO approach which states accountability as well as desired results. Moreover, one-man accountability (e.g., holding only the chief executive responsible for the performance of the total enterprise) should be replaced by multiple levels of accountability.

McConkey, D. D. "Results Approach to Evaluating Managerial Performance." *Advanced Management Journal* 32 (October 1967): 18–26.

The focus of this discussion is on managing by objectives, measuring by objectives, and developing objectives for successive levels within an organization. The author also discusses some of the problems that may arise when MBO is implemented in only part (e.g., a department) of an organization.

McConkey, D. D. "Writing Measurable Objectives for Staff Managers." *Advanced Management Journal* 37 (January 1972): 10–16.

The staff manager must give considerable thought to his true mission in the organization before he can write worthwhile and meaningful objectives. Failure to do so usually results in a list of routine activities he plans to pursue. In this article, the author provides some guidelines and illustrations to help the staff manager (1) determine his mission, (2) move from qualitative to more quantitative objectives, and (3) make them more concrete and specific.

McConkey, D. D. "Implementation: The Guts of MBO." *Advanced Management Journal* 37 (July 1972): 13–18.

After examining the successes and failures of MBO programs, the author suggests that the answer lies in the manner in which the system is implemented. He provides some questions to be answered before implementing MBO and some guidelines to be followed during and after its implementation. Several suggestions concerning the use of consultants are also provided.

McConkey, D. D. "20 Ways to Kill Management By Objectives." *Management Review* 61 (October 1972): 4–13.

In this article, the author provides a list of twenty ways to kill even the best MBO program. They range from creating a paper mill, to ignoring feedback, to being impatient, to omitting periodic reviews, to refusing to delegate to subordinates. He concludes that highly competent managers are required to operate an MBO system effectively.

McGregor, Douglas. "An Uneasy Look at Performance Appraisal." *Harvard Business Review* 35 (May-June 1957): 89–94.

The conventional approach to performance appraisal is condemned as a violation of the "integrity of the personality" by this late behavioral scientist. It places the manager in the uncomfortable and untenable position of judging the personal worth of his subordinates, and not only acting upon these judgments, but communicating them to those he has judged. No manager has the skill required to carry out this responsibility effectively. Few would even be willing to accept it if they were fully aware of the implications of "playing God." According to the author, MBO offers a sounder approach to performance appraisal. It places the major responsibility for establishing performance goals and appraising progress toward them on the subordinate, avoids the problems of the conventional approach, and stimulates the growth and development of subordinates.

Mackay, John A. H. "Management By Objective in the Canada Post Office." *Canadian Personnel* 18 (January 1971): 13–17.

This is a description of the application of MBO in the Canadian Post Office. Its implementation involves the use of a catalyst group, consisting of a small number of business-oriented managers from industry, as a vehicle for teaching the mechanics of "business planning" (MBO) to selected senior managers of the Post Office. These selected managers and catalysts then work with other managers and supervisors to assist in the application of MBO.

Mendelson, Jack L. "Goal Setting: An Important Management Tool." *Arizona Business Bulletin* (May 1968): 121–27.

The focus of this article is on the nature and purpose of goal-setting in organizations, as well as on some of the key issues which must be considered with its use. Among other things, the author tentatively concludes (1) that the process involves work planning in addition to the mere setting of goals, (2) that primary emphasis should be placed on short-run rather than long-run results, (3) that individual goals, rather than group goals, should be given first attention, and (4) that explicit superior-subordinate interaction around the subordinate's personal goals tends to strengthen goal-setting efforts.

Mendelson, Jack L. "Personal Targets for Effective Management." *Canadian Business* (January 1970): 9–13.

Individual Goal Setting (IGS) is described by the author as a process of establishing individual work goals for a specific time period. Although his superior plays an active role, the individual himself has the initiating responsibility. This encourages his growth toward self-direction at a pace which is reasonable for him.

Meyer, H. H., E. Kay, and J. R. P. French, Jr. "Split Roles in Performance Appraisal." *Harvard Business Review* 43 (January-February 1965): 123–29.

Research conducted at the General Electric Company is reported in this article. The "traditional" performance appraisal program was found to have many shortcomings causing the company to introduce their Work Planning and Review (WPR) system. The authors describe the experiment and conclude that the new WPR program proved to be considerably more effective than the traditional approach.

Meyers, M. Scott. "Conditions for Manager Motivation." *Harvard Business Review* 44 (January-February 1966): 58–71.

The author isolates three conditions under which managers and subordinates were found to be motivated at Texas Instruments, Inc. These include (1) the interpersonal skill and managerial style of the superior, (2) an opportunity to work toward meaningful goals, and (3) a suitable management system. The author's description of the T.I. goal-setting approach includes a discussion of the delegation process, the administrative climate, and the de-emphasis of status symbols. Among the five management systems discussed are a work simplification program and a performance review system.

Murray, Richard K. "Behavioral Management Objectives." *Personnel Journal* 52 (April 1973): 304–6.

Effective management objectives, according to this author, contain three elements. These include (1) a statement of the specific results to be attained in behavioral terms, (2) a statement of a specific time frame (i.e., when the objective will be accomplished), and (3) a statement of a specific criterion which can be used to evaluate performance. Illustrations and guidelines are also provided.

Patten, Thomas H. "O.D., MBO and the R/P Systems: A New Dimension in Personnel Administration." *Personnel Administration* 35 (March-April 1972): 14–26.

The focus of this article is on integrating organizational development (OD), management by objectives (MBO), and the reward and penalty (R/P) system. After a brief description of each, the author presents a number of alternative ways to integrate them and describes some of the potential problems. He argues for an "optimum" strategy which involves introducing OD before the implementation of MBO and the subsequent revamping of the R/P system.

Patton, Arch. "How to Appraise Executive Performance." *Harvard Business Review* 38 (January-February 1960): 63–70.

After a brief review of some of the weaknesses of the earlier approaches to appraisal, the author cites a number of advantages to be gained by "planned performance." A detailed description of this MBO process and illustrations of planned performance targets for various managerial positions are also provided. Some of the features of this approach include: (1) The long- and short-term objectives of the company become an integral part of the process; (2) executive job responsibilities provide the basis for setting individual targets; (3) the outstanding and poor performers receive primary attention; and (4) personality plays a less important part in the final evaluation of executive performance.

Raia, Anthony P. "Goal-Setting and Self-Control." *Journal of Management Studies* 2 (February 1965): 35–53.

The Purex Corporation's "Goals and Controls" approach to MBO is studied in an attempt to assess its impact on organization performance. Among the major advantages found by the author after eighteen months of implementation are better planning at the operating plant level, improved problem-solving at each managerial level, a basis for more objectivity in performance appraisal, and improved communications between the geographically separated plants and company headquarters. Some potential problem areas were also noted. The author concludes that neither its apparent success nor its problems can be attributed to any specific aspect of the program, but rather to the extent to which the MBO philosophy has been practiced by the participants.

Raia, Anthony P. "A Second Look at Goals and Controls." *California Management Review* 8 (Summer 1966): 49–58.

This is essentially a re-examination and re-appraisal of the Purex program a year after the author's initial study. He concludes that the impact of the "Goals and Controls" program continues to be favorable. Despite its apparent success, however, a number of problems remain unsolved. These include (1) a distortion in the managerial philosophy underlying the program, (2) the lack of participation at the lower levels of the organization, (3) an increase in paperwork, (4) an over-emphasis on production-oriented goals, and (5) the lack of incentive and motivation to maintain a high level of commitment among participating managers.

Raia, Anthony P. "Management By Objectives: In Theory and Practice." *Southern Journal of Business* (January 1968): 11–20.

In this article the author discusses the theory underlying the MBO approach to management and describes its application at Purex.

The discussion includes a description of the "Goals and Controls" program and how it was implemented by this company. Some of the findings and conclusions of his two earlier studies are also briefly discussed.

Ross, Robert D. "New Dimensions for Public Relations with Management By Objectives." *Advanced Management Journal* 37 (July 1972): 36–42.

This is a general description of and rationale for MBO in the public relations function of an organization. The focus is on developing objectives which are aimed at solving PR "problems." A step-by-step process, guidelines, and illustrations are provided.

Scheid, Phil N. "Charter of Accountability for Executives." *Harvard Business Review* 43 (July-August 1965): 88–98.

This is a description of a management system labelled COACH, an acronym for "Charter of Accountability Concept–Hughes." According to the author, this approach calls for the establishment of written "charters" for each major division of the organization. Each charter of accountability contains (1) a statement of purpose, (2) a listing of important objectives, (3) a breakdown of the functional accountabilities necessary to accomplish the objectives, and (4) a subseries of target tasks which provide middle managers with definitive targets.

Schollhammer, Hans. "Executive Progress Review." *Management International Review* (1968): 87–93 (UCLA Reprint 118).

Some of the "traditional" performance appraisal schemes are reviewed and their disadvantages noted by the author. Executive Progress Review, according to him, involves setting performance targets and developing action programs for their attainment. The evaluation process emphasizes a problem-solving approach whereby results are measured, deviations noted, and justifications for discrepancies are stated. The author also discusses a number of other aspects related to the program.

Sloan, Stanley, and David E. Schrieber. "What We Need to Know About MBO." *Personnel Journal* 49 (March 1970): 206–8.

According to the authors, there are insufficient knowledge and follow-up studies on the effectiveness of MBO as a management technique. They raise a number of questions and suggest areas of research to help fill the knowledge gaps.

Tosi, H. L., Jr. "Management Development and Management By Objectives—An Interrelationship." *Management of Personnel Quarterly* 4 (Summer 1965): 21–27.

There is a close relationship between management development and MBO. Although management development does not necessarily include MBO, according to the author, MBO is a vehicle for developing managers. He discusses some of the aspects of managing by objectives and various considerations for its implementation.

Tosi, H. L., Jr., and S. J. Carroll. "Management Reaction to Management By Objectives." *Academy of Management Journal* 11 (December 1968): 415–26.

Some 48 managers were interviewed in an attempt to evaluate the impact of a Work Planning and Review program. The advantages cited by the authors are fairly consistent with those of earlier studies including an increase in certainty about job requirements, greater satisfaction with appraisal criteria, and forcing communication between superiors and subordinates. The problems encountered are also similar to those found in other studies. In addition, the authors found that the degree of top management involvement, support, and reinforcement has an impact on the way in which subordinates react to and use the program. Constant review is needed to ensure that the program fills a legitimate need which operating managers sense exists.

Tosi, H. L., Jr., and S. J. Carroll. "Some Structural Factors to Goal Influence in the MBO Process." *MSU Business Topics* 17 (Spring 1969): 45–50.

The focus of this report is on the influence of participants on performance goals in a WPR program. The authors suggest that the degree of influence is related to functional areas as well as to organizational levels. Moreover, four kinds of goal-setting processes are identified and related to an influence index. Introducing an MBO program may not only require a change in policy, according to them, but may also require complex organizational changes.

Tosi, H. L., Jr., and S. J. Carroll. "Some Factors Affecting the Success of Management By Objectives." *Journal of Management Studies* 7 (May 1970): 209–23.

In this report, based on their study of a WPR program in a large manufacturing firm, the authors suggest that the process should be flexible and should consider the characteristics of participating subordinates. However, they conclude that further research is necessary to provide more definite answers.

Tosi, H. L., Jr., and S. J. Carroll. "Management By Objectives." *Personnel Administration* 33 (July-August 1970): 44–48.

This is essentially a description of the basic aspects of MBO and some of its potential advantages and problem areas. The authors stress that the program must be relevant and must receive organizational support if it is to succeed. One way in which this can be done, they conclude, is to link it to other elements of the system which reinforce behavior, such as compensation and rewards.

Tosi, H. L., Jr., John R. Rizzo, and S. J. Carroll. "Setting Goals in Management By Objectives." *California Management Review* 7 (Summer 1970): 70–78.

This is essentially a restatement, in language that can be understood by the practicing manager, of many of the research findings reported by the authors in some of their earlier writings on the subject. In this article they discuss the focus, purpose, and process of managing by and with objectives. A number of useful guidelines are provided for establishing objectives, developing an action plan for their accomplishment, and providing for measurement and appraisal at the end of the cycle. The importance of top management support and involvement in the process is stressed throughout their descriptions.

Valentine, Raymond F. "Laying the Groundwork for Goal-setting." *Personnel* 43 (January-February 1966): 34–41.

Before superior and subordinate meet to agree on performance goals, according to this author, it is up to the boss to do the preliminary thinking needed to arrive at targets and yardsticks that are meaningful for all concerned. This requires the superior to become familiar with company goals for the period, as well as the basic functional responsibilities of his subordinate.

Wade, M. "Only Way to Manage (By Objectives)." *Business Management* (July 1967): 34–39.

This is a discussion of the application of MBO in two companies. In one company, the program was started at the top. In the other it was started at the departmental level. The author suggests that MBO is not just another management gimmick, but rather allows the manager to plan and work as a professional.

Wall, Richard H. "Reconciling Organization and Personal Goals." *Personnel Journal* 49 (January 1970): 41–44.

Changes in the external and internal environment, according to the author, generally require adjustments in organizational behavior. He suggests a number of experimental questions designed to promote a climate of mutual support in the goal-setting process.

Wickens, J. D. "MBO: An Appraisal." *Journal of Management Studies* 5 (October 1968): 365–79.

There are some limitations, according to this author, to the universal application of MBO. A number of earlier attempts to establish the approach in British organizations failed because it did not become institutionalized. The author provides a review and analysis of some of the theory of organizational behavior as the basis for describing a case study. The focus of his description is generally on the interrelatedness of human motivation, the technological environment, and management practices. He concludes that MBO may be universally applicable provided that the organization structure and management practices are modified to facilitate its implementation, and provided that an appropriate "psychological model" is used.

Wilkerson, David C. "A Results-Oriented Development Plan." *The Conference Board Record* 3 (March 1966): 40–45.

This article discusses the "Development Bank" approach of the research and engineering division of the Kimberly-Clark Corporation. The "Development Bank" involves a program that provides for self-development that is related to the needs and objectives of the company. The program is the result of the company's experience with MBO.

Wikstrom, Walter S. "MBO or Appraisal by Results." *The Conference Board Review* (July 1966): 27–31.

A distinction is made between appraisal by results and management by objectives. The author considers the former to be a performance appraisal technique, and the latter a vehicle which stresses planning, organizing, motivating, and controlling. The problems and benefits of each approach are discussed in some detail.

Index

196

1 4 6 2 5   4